Entrepreneurial Empire

Navigating the Complexities of Entrepreneurship

Jacqueline N. Hernandez

Publishing Group or Company products/services. Earnings potentials is entirely dependent on the efforts, skills and application of the individual person. Exercises and ideas in the information materials offered are simply opinion or experience, and thus should not be misinterpreted as promises, typical results or guarantees (expressed or implied). The author and the publisher Jacqueline Hernández, IME Publishing Group (IME or any IME Representatives) Shall in no way, under any circumstances be held liable to any party (or third-party) for any direct, indirect, punitive, special, incidental or other consequential damages arising directly or indirectly from any use of books, materials and or seminar trainings, which is provided "as is," and without warranties Jacqueline Hernandez/IME Publishing Group.

Any examples, stories, references, or case studies are for illustrative purposes only and should not be interpreted as testimonies and/or examples of what reader and/or consumers are generally expected from the information. No representation in any part of this information, materials and/ or seminar trainings are guarantees or promises for actual performance. Any statements, strategies, concepts, techniques, exercises and ideas in the information materials and/or seminar training offered are simply opinion or experience, and thus should not be misinterpreted as promises, typical results or guarantees (expressed or implied). The author and the publisher (Jacqueline Hernández, IME Publishing Group (IME) or any IME Representatives) Shall in no way, under any circumstances be held liable to any party (or third-party) for any direct, indirect, punitive, special, incidental or other consequential damages arising directly or indirectly from any use of books, materials and or seminar trainings, which is provided "as is," and without warranties Jacqueline Hernández/IME Publishing Group.

IME Publishing Group
1990 N California Blvd. Suite 20 PMB 1065
Walnut Creek, California 94596
1-866-726-6563
www.IMEPublishingGroup.com
Jacqueline Hernández-1st ed.

i/Me
PUBLISHING GROUP
INSPIRE-MOTIVATE-EMPOWER

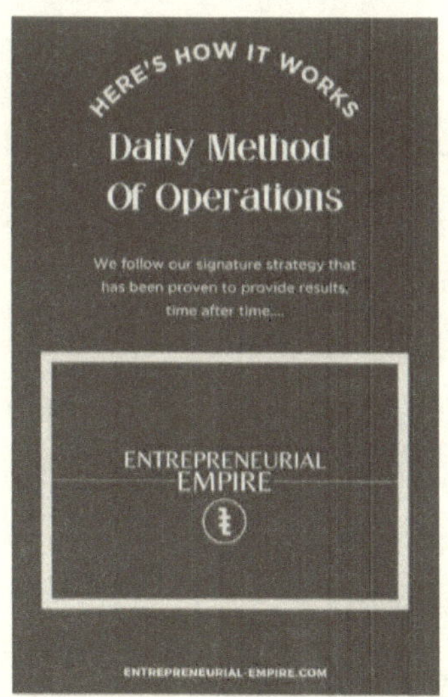

https://bit.ly/-DMO

Table of Contents

Acknowledgments 1

Preface 5

[CH 1] The Author's Article: The Making of an Entrepreneur 13

[CH 2] Laying the Groundwork: Setting the Stage for Success 19

[CH 3] Strategy Unleashed: Analyze, Blueprint, and Cohesion 29

[CH 4] Target Your N.I.C.H.E. 47

[CH 5] Breakthrough in Pricing 63

[CH 6] Authentic Branding: Unicorn in the Marketspace 73

[CH 7] Beyond Illusions: Embracing the Grit and Setbacks of Entrepreneurhood 85

[CH 8] Paving the Path to Scaling Success 97

[CH 9] Partnerships Built to Last 111

[CH 10] Igniting Your Entrepreneurial Journey 129

About the Author 137

Acknowledgments

Throughout this journey as an entrepreneur, I have most definitely experienced the good, the bad, the ugly and then the great. The people that have supported me in this uphill challenge were unwavering in their belief in me and my superpowers. I want to first thank my dad, Gilbert Hernandez, for developing in me a bulletproof CONFIDENCE and always believing in me. It's because of this confidence and belief that I have been able to get into rooms and situations that elevated my learning and experience with industry icons. Dad, you are the maker of leaders. The second special appreciation is for my step-mom Debbie Hernandez, as I navigated through being a single mom and taking on an entrepreneurial career, she showed up as a support to help with my kids, allowing me to join opportunities I would not be available for if it wasn't for her. She taught me patience and parental responsibilities.

To my Aunt Mela Aquino, who always gave me sound advice and never just agreed with me, she helped me see things from a different lens. She is the person I run to when I need strength and an unbiased point of view. As an entrepreneur, my Aunt Mela's role in my life would keep me grounded and my ego in check. Everyone needs someone in their life that will tell them what they need to hear, not just what they want to hear. She has become one of my favorite people in life, smart, strong, and a confidant.

My two older children, Victoria and Gilbert, thank you for your patience, your resilience, and leaning into us as a family through the struggle. We overcame this together, you two, are both champions in our family's success. I am truly blessed with you both. I also want to thank my daughter-in-law Ivania Hernandez for pushing me to finish this book. Thank you for the daily encouragement and your friendship most importantly.

Big appreciation for my three younger children Marciano, Acacia and Aveya, you are the very reason why I am able to accomplish as much as I have. Because I am your mom, I have to be the best version of myself and show up every day for you. Everything I do, I do it with you in mind. I love you all with so much abundance. All five of you, as my children, have helped to shape this journey in your own individual ways. There have been times that I have received the best sound advice from our discussions when facing a problem ahead. Most importantly, thank you for your honesty when it comes to our family and decisions that affect our family publicly and privately, along with our future goals. Every single one of you has inspired me more than you could ever know.

To my partner in life, Jacob Salazar, thank you for coming into my life, joining my family and being a friend and role model to my five kids. As an entrepreneur you have seen me face many challenges and you were there in my weakest moments helping me figure it out, reminding me that I am a "boss baddie." You show up for me every time, you have taken on a lot of my business challenges and mastered them all so I can succeed. You are my hero, my champion, and my better half. The calm to my many storms.

There are so many others that I want to thank, my mom Mary, for giving me the experience to make decisions and run a business at such a young age. That exposure set the tone for my career and the ability to never settle, but to create. My Aunt Sylvia and late Uncle Larry Vigil, for grooming me to run organizations, and for being my first mentors, instilling me the characteristics of what a leader is. It's because of you, my spirituality is solid, and my faith is second to none.

Last but not least, my coach Mike Driggers, you are the best coach there is and you inspire me every day to take action. This book would not be possible without your guidance. You truly are the Leader's Leader.

Preface

Navigating the Complexities **of Entrepreneurship:** Many entrepreneurs find themselves in a maze of uncertainty, not knowing where to turn for guidance. The intricacies of starting, scaling, and sustaining a business can be overwhelming, leaving the entrepreneur searching for a clear path forward. In this book, we will dive into these three core benefits, providing actionable insights, real-world examples, and practical exercises to help you transform your entrepreneurial journey. Each chapter is designed to address specific entrepreneurial setbacks, equipping you with the knowledge and tools to overcome challenges and build an entrepreneurial empire that thrives regardless of the economic landscape.

My entrepreneurial journey has been a testament to transforming old ways of doing things into something revolutionary. I, too, faced the daunting task of navigating the complexities of entrepreneurship. The struggle was real, and the road was fraught with uncertainties. It's through these trials and tribulations that I developed the blueprint outlined in this book.

Starting Point

In the heart of Silicon Valley, amidst the relentless waves of innovation, I was immersed in the tumultuous world of business. I watched as companies soared to unprecedented heights and, sadly, witnessed others stumble and fall. It was within this crucible of experience that the invaluable lessons shaping this book were born.

As a seasoned business development consultant, I lead with a hands-on, in-the-trenches approach that has honed my problem-solving skills. I've crafted tailor-made solutions for businesses across diverse industries at every phase of their journey. Just like any entrepreneur, I didn't start off with clarity, rather more from a place of necessity. My entrepreneurial journey first began a staggering seventeen years ago when I ventured into the realm of home-based businesses, also known as network marketing. To be clear, let me just say at the onset, network marketing is no walk in the park. General consensus would claim that it is darn near impossible to make any real income, and that you must rely heavily on your ability to shine, while becoming lined with thick skin. To truly succeed, one must approach it with unwavering dedication and the mindset that it can replace the conventional 9-to-5 grind to offer you more income and a better life. I saw most people fail because of their approach, they either worked it like it was a cute hobby, or they hustled it like their lives depended on it. I recognized that to be the differentiator within the industry's parameters between success and failure.

My most transformative experience in network marketing came when I realized that the conventional playbook no longer sufficed. I embraced a fresh perspective thinking outside the box, one that prioritized strategic planning, innovative problem-solving, and the power of authentic branding. These paradigm shifts revolutionized my entrepreneurial journey within the network marketing space. Taking me from zero to hero. Within eighteen months of this mindset shift I was able to accomplish hitting the second to the last highest paid position in the entire company. New doors began to unlock and swing wide open, elevating me into leadership retreats, company decision making, and mentorship with the owners of the company. The opportunities to learn about strategic planning and the future of the company were eye-opening.

Turning Point

The network marketing company I was established with was a telecommunications company called ACN. They provided wholesale pricing for phone lines and cell phones. They forged a partnership with none other than Donald Trump himself. As a celebrity and leader in the business world, his endorsement to the company was explosive. He would attend our events, delivering keynote speeches that unpacked the intricacies of business strategies, the power of mindset, and the hard lessons learned from failure. Trump openly shared his experiences, including his brush with bankruptcy involving millions of dollars, and how he emerged stronger from failure.

The pinnacle of this partnership came when we, the top-performing representatives, received a coveted invitation. We were invited to attend the filming of The Apprentice Season 8, Episode 4, titled "Failure to

Negotiate" in 2008. This event was nothing short of extraordinary. We flew out to New York City, enjoyed dinner with the celebrities on the show and learned about the marketing plan each team had in store for us. We were given the esteemed title of guest judges, entrusted with the responsibility of determining the fate of the celebrity teams. Both teams were tasked with using our company's flagship product, the video phone (this was before the iPhone launched facetime). They did a remarkable job with product market fit, but in the end, only one team won. A staggering 85% of our votes were cast in favor of the KOTU team, making our impact undeniable and a part of television network history.

Unlocking New Horizons

Through the company's partnership with Donald Trump, my own perspective underwent a profound transformation. I began to perceive fresh opportunities to extend my experience with ACN and use it as guidance to local business owners and aspiring entrepreneurs grappling with challenges. Armed with techniques to conquer adversity and keep their businesses afloat, I became their unwavering support, cheerleader, strategic advisor and coach. I would hang up my leadership empire with ACN to forge a new path that widened a much larger purpose in Business Consultancy. I was now able to help everyone with a dream of building a business by tapping into their innate talents and specialized skills. Broadening the horizon.

Career Transition

My journey through network marketing became a profound school of entrepreneurship. Personally, building a team of over 6,000 independent representatives across North America instilled in me the invaluable qualities of mentorship, rigorous training, unyielding responsibility, taking ownership, late hours and the unwavering mindset that the future was mine to shape.

This journey set the stage for my transition into the realm of business development consultancy. My mission was clear: to make a meaningful impact on the lives of entrepreneurs. I aspired to offer coaching and advisory services that not only ensured their survival in the business world but also empowered them to construct empires capable of enduring for generations. The industry of network marketing had granted me the unique opportunity to master every facet of business and impart this knowledge in a way that positioned business owners I worked with as the unrivaled unicorns of their industries.

Today, as an entrepreneur, coach, advisor, and business development consultant, I've had the privilege of working with thousands of entrepreneurs across North America, implementing the blueprint and methods detailed in this book. My sphere of influence extends to Fortune 100 companies, government agencies, non-profits, small businesses, churches, and ultra-affluent families, guiding them to establish themselves as the foremost authorities in their respective industries, even amidst ever-evolving landscapes.

Expectations

In the chapters ahead, I'm excited to share these transformative insights with you. You'll uncover the art of confidently navigating the complexities of entrepreneurship, the magic of crafting an authentic brand that resonates deeply, and the secrets to forging enduring partnerships.

In a world saturated with businesses vying for attention, standing out and building an authentic brand can be a formidable challenge. Unfortunately, entrepreneurs often struggle to define their unique value proposition and connect with their target audience in a meaningful way.

As we discover the art of authentic branding and how to distinguish your business in a competitive market you will find yourself connecting the dots with your authenticity and product market fit much easier. Those aha moments that we long for will present themselves in this book. Together, we will uncover strategies to connect with your audience on a profound level, creating a brand that resonates and compels loyalty.

We will also look for ways to work smarter not harder by using exponential growth versus singular growth. Building and maintaining strong alliances can be a daunting task. Entrepreneurs frequently encounter hurdles in forming partnerships that endure and contribute to their business acceleration.

We will address how masterful partnership building can harness the power of a strategic movement through proven techniques. Learn how to forge alliances that endure, amplify your resources, and open doors to new opportunities, all while avoiding common pitfalls that hinder collaborative success.

The Entrepreneurial Empire Blueprint isn't just a collection of strategies; it's a revolutionary guide that empowers you to conquer the ever-evolving landscape of entrepreneurship. So, let's embark on this journey together, and I'll show you how to turn the old way of doing things into a revolutionizing force that propels your entrepreneurial empire to unprecedented heights.

[CH 1] The Author's Article: The Making of an Entrepreneur

I have been in the business development industry for seventeen years now and I am still going strong. However, my first taste of entrepreneurhood dates back to when I was in my early teens. My mom owned a coffee spot at the famous racetrack in Berkeley, California known as The Golden Gate Fields. It was a busy place filled with clouds of smoke and peanut shells all over the floor, the habits of the gamblers inhabited the arena in its entirety.

As a thirteen-year-old I got an up-close and personal view of human behavior. The racetrack had a mixed bag of characters for sure, there were businessmen meeting together in the box seats, senior citizen groups that came to socialize with each other and hang out all day. Then you would see the loners that would grip their tickets with a nervousness running over them, pacing the stadium floor waiting to win big. I once witnessed a man pass out, falling straight to the floor because he placed a bet on a losing horse using his entire paycheck. My mom had a pretty cool partnership with the racetrack, I got to listen in on her conversations as she negotiated her terms and conditions to set up her coffee spot.

My mom was an entrepreneur by nature, business savvy, who had an eye for opportunity and incredibly talented. She was also a woman who struggled with health issues, preventing her from applying her full attention to her business at times. I saw in her the drive and ambition of an entrepreneur up close and admired her strength to persevere during the hard times in life. Her attitude "if it is meant to be, it's up to me!" stuck with me in everything I would set out to do in my future.

It was in these challenging times my mom would ask me to run the whole coffee business by myself. I would spend my whole summer there hustling coffee; this was before Starbucks was a household name and the coffee business was just a dull pot of coffee served at restaurants in a generic cup. My mom struck a deal with me, she said "if you go and work this for me, you can keep half of the profit after everything is paid to run the business." Who can say no to that! I sure didn't, I was all in. When I say all in, I came up with ways to get people to change their buying habits from a simple cup of joe to a full-blown cappuccino, latte, Mocha, white mocha and americanos (espresso topped with water), yes, a fancier coffee at a higher price. I gave away samples, walked up to people, had conversations about their day, got interested in their families and learned about what brought them out to the track.

The coffee spot was a hit, before I knew it, I had regulars who waited in line for me to open up so they could get their coffee first. Customers liked me so much they requested that I have a tip jar out. As a thirteen-year-old, tips were a new concept for me. I put one out as suggested and I couldn't believe the tips I received. People would leave $10 tips that weren't even spending that much for their coffee order. I asked the police officer who would always stand by my area, why someone would leave a bigger tip than their actual cost. His words verbatim, "Because they like you kid. You're the sunshine to life's gloom." I never forgot the lesson I learned from that.

Now that the word was out, and the attendees loved us, it eventually became too much for me to handle alone. I had to employ a friend to help out with the growing demand. I had to decide what I would pay her, what was fair, and train her in the daily routine, along with customer service. I learned a lot at that racetrack, most importantly I saw the importance of observation and staying consistent. I have to say, my teenage upbringing was a bit unconventional, which I believe unleashed the creativity and visionary spirit within me.

Take Action

Looking back on your younger years, what experience shifted a light onto entrepreneurhood for you? What did you learn from it? Write it down.

Notes

Notes

[CH 2] Laying the Groundwork: Setting the Stage for Success

In the world of Entrepreneurial Empire, we believe in beginning with the end in mind, to understand that it is crucial in conveying this message to the entrepreneurs we work with. It is not uncommon for entrepreneurs to set out on their business ventures with grand visions and innovative ideas, but without a clear understanding of what it takes to turn those ideas into successful empires, is often where they find themselves in trouble. Many aspiring entrepreneurs, eager to save capital and cut corners, often underestimate the importance of proper planning and investing in the right areas of their business.

Let's explore two key factors that can determine an entrepreneur's success. First, would be the danger of choosing cheapness over value and second would be the misleading nature of busyness as a measure of progress.

By understanding and avoiding these two traps, entrepreneurs can achieve sustainable growth and build a remarkable brand in this competitive, ever-changing market.

The Pitfall of Being Cheap

One of the biggest mistakes entrepreneurs make is trying to be cheap in all the wrong areas of their business strategy. They underestimate the true cost of cutting corners and will end up paying a hefty price in the long run. Building a business on a shoestring budget without the proper investment in critical areas can lead to subpar results. In some cases, improper usage of the business budget can cause failure before it even launches. It is crucial for entrepreneurs to understand that being cheap can and will cost them their entire business and hinder their chances of building a sustainable empire.

I can't tell you how many times I've been brought aboard a project as the last hope, the final straw that might, or might not break the camel's back. It's mind boggling to see entrepreneurs drive themselves crazy, going in circles, even coming close to flatlining their businesses. They will go through all of that before they seek out the valued help that was needed from the very beginning. They will hit the consumer streets to start hustling their product and start attracting sales. But that's as far as they can get, they don't have the systems and plans in place to retain customers or scale the growth. How you do one thing is how you do everything, and if first impressions are lasting, what impression are you making by not being fully prepared.

Case Study

There are so many steps that need to take place before you launch your business and open it to customers. I had someone that was referred to me by a friend, let's call this referral Fred. Before I met with Fred I had him fill out my intake form. On the form I asked questions like:

- How much have you invested so far? And how much do you have now to invest?

- Who do you have working with you that has specialized expertise?

- Have you ever worked with a consultant or a business development coach before?

- What do you currently use for CRM?

- Who does your marketing?

- What do your current reviews and testimonials look like?

- What are your frustrations?

- What is the timeline for your completion?

I had a conversation with Fred, after he submitted his intake form regarding his needs, concerns for his business and what he wanted to accomplish with my help. I could tell the business was in bad shape based on his tone of voice and posture. I began with my initial assessment and designed a roadmap for his succession planning. I walked him through the process step by step and explained to him what needed to happen for him to achieve optimal results. He loved this plan so much that his melancholy demeanor perked up. He asked me if I could email him the elaborate roadmap I created. He told me he wanted to get better acquainted with the details in it. I got the sense that he was going to go at it alone. And just as my gut feeling predicted, a few days later Fred sent me an email letting me know he decided against my services, writing that he had figured out a solution to his needs.

About four months later I got an email from Fred, asking if I could zoom meet with him at my earliest convenience. At our meeting, he explained to me how his business was still in the same state it was when we last talked. It turns out he didn't think it was worth the money to pay me for my help. He stated that he saw the outline I gave him as "good advice" and that he could have easily learned this from a book or friend. He looked at the roadmap I created and concluded he had all the answers to his problems now at his fingertips. Fred was convinced that all he had to do was apply the action items to his business for his success to turn around.

It wasn't that Fred needed the answers to his business to become successful, it was that Fred needed the experience of every component on that roadmap. And since Fred did not have SEO, CRM, marketing, social media, google review, campaigning, email journey, website, digital excitement videos, copyright, PM tools and ad experience, he was still at a loss. Fred was good at his specific product, no wait, I take that back, Fred was incredibly talented at his product. Millionaire status talented. I told Fred, my job is to keep him focused on his lane of expertise and let others do the things he's not good at or shouldn't be spending his time doing. Fred finally hired me and has been doing amazing things ever since.

Let me share a little secret with you: many of my clients prefer to keep our consulting help and coaching under wraps by signing a non-disclosure agreement

(NDA). They value their reputation and fear that others might snatch away their business if they knew about the support they received. But let me tell you something—I consider that mentality to be outdated and rooted in scarcity.

Personally, I've always been an advocate for sharing resources and uplifting others who have contributed to my success. I firmly believe in abundance, and I have unwavering confidence in my authentic authority. You see, authentic authority is what sets you apart and draws your audience especially to you. It's a topic I will dive into in chapter 5.

Entrepreneurs, Listen Up

Investing in the right kind of help from the very beginning is non-negotiable. Trust me when I say that trying to save a few bucks will only come back to haunt you. I've had countless clients come to me, relieved that I took the time to assess their situation and lay it all out on the table with a realistic approach based on their actual skills. What is my coaching mantra? Results. Results that are tailor-made for your business and generate serious revenue. If I can't deliver high-level results, I won't work with you. It's as simple as that.

But it's not just about promising the moon and the stars. I believe in transparency and clarity, which is why I provide my clients with a detailed proposal that outlines every step of the process and the outcomes they can expect. When they can visualize the journey ahead, they become active participants rather than resistant roadblocks.

Now, let me be clear: Don't just read this book and start randomly searching the web or social media for help. Do your research, ask around, and find the right consulting company or coach for you. Because let me tell you, getting involved with the wrong people can be just as costly as trying to go at it alone.

So, entrepreneurs, it's time to step up and invest in the right kind of help. Let's turn your business into the success story you've always envisioned.

The Illusion of Busyness: Entrepreneurs often fall into the trap of equating busy-ness with productivity. They work tirelessly, dedicating long hours to their business, yet fail to generate meaningful results. The key is to focus on productive actions that yield tangible outcomes rather than merely being busy. When you take the time to analyze your business analytics and assess the actual results produced by their efforts, will prove itself vital for entrepreneurs to understand whether they are moving in the right direction or need to adjust.

Back to the Case Study

Fred was so busy; he would be the first to tell you the words "burnt out" would flash through his mind. In fact, he was drained to the point of giving up. I am proud of Fred, who had the guts to admit he needed help and for his honesty when it came to his confession to me about why he didn't hire me the first time. I discovered that while Fred was working on his product. He was also taking classes to design banners for social media posts. He was also learning how to use email journeying and bought a CRM but didn't know how to use it, so he was taking class and scouring YouTube to learn how to use these essentials. He started going to networking meetings to meet new people to talk about his product. Fred told me this was a challenge for him because he didn't have business cards and never designed his website to a level that he would want to give it out to people and his social media looked like something out of the 90's.

Fred was definitely busy. He was trying hard to be the jack of all trades but master of none. Fred is just one example of hundreds of people I talk to about this, who do the very thing Fred was doing. Imagine you're wanting to play baseball because you're the best batter, you can hit the ball so hard it flies out of the stadium. You start running around spreading the news for people all over town to come watch the game you're playing in. Game day arrives and you're excited, you're lit. You are about to drop jaws when people see you swing. Batters up... that's you. First problem, you never employed a pitcher, so now this role falls on you, you're the pitcher, and the batter. Okay a little hiccup, but you managed to throw the ball in the air and hit it way into the outfield. Next problem, you don't have an outfielder, so you must run out there to retrieve the ball. Since you're not a good runner, you walk quickly to the ball. Time is going by, and your audience is growing bored, they all know how the game of baseball is run to know this experience is not how it's supposed to go. So, your audience begins to boo, and leave. Thank God they didn't pay to watch this one man show, just think of the angry mob that would have developed and the amount of refunds that would be requested. In this scenario, the batter is the expert, who is now spending his time running around doing other duties because he didn't employ a team and the customers are the impatient mob of people that are feeling you should have had it all together before you invited them out for this.

Customers can be brutal when their experience with you is sub-par.

Take Action

How can you avoid being the solo player on a baseball team?

Write down what your current struggles are and outline what strategies you have implemented. Now determine your results.

Ask yourself, are you doing the same thing over and over and expecting different results?

Look into joining a business coaching program that fits your budget and your needs.

Notes

Notes

[CH 3] Strategy Unleashed: Analyze, Blueprint, and Cohesion

The Need for a Good Strategy

When entrepreneurs approach me to fix the mess they find themselves in, it often stems from a lack of improper planning and mapping out their business strategy. Without a well-defined plan, entrepreneurs can easily find themselves going in the wrong direction without realizing it. Often, they won't catch the derailed course they're on until they are too far off from their desired destination, or even worse they can be too far down the road to fix the chaos.

Correcting the course of a business requires time, effort, and a comprehensive understanding of the steps involved. It is crucial for entrepreneurs to acknowledge and embrace the need for a clear strategy from the outset.

Strategy is a term that gets thrown around in business circles as a way to impress folks. Everyone wants to talk about strategy but can't identify the core components of what a good one is. Some of the strategies I've heard remind me of Swiss cheese, the substance is there, with a lot of gaps. Not everyone understands the true essence of strategy.

Thinking back to my first run in with strategy reminds me of when I stayed with my Aunt Sylvia and Uncle Larry, who were regional pastors of a church in Oakland, California. Living with them gave me a 24/7 insight into leading with vision, planning and strategy. They were part of a church organization whose mission was to share the message of God to the ghettos of America. The headquarter church launched an audacious plan to send out 2,000 churches by the year 2000 and opened their parameters globally. They designed a plan to train couples who would become the pastors of these churches that would launch into every major city throughout the world.

While most pre-teens spent their summers playing outside, I spent my formidable years in strategy sessions and leadership trainings. I listened and observed my aunt and uncle instill the vision within their congregation, develop a solid plan that involved research, scouting out geographical areas to launch a baby church, identifying which couple would be best suited for which city, and the capital they would need to raise for each church to get launched successfully. I got a front row seat to what a good strategy looked like, and what it didn't look like. I had the VIP backstage passes to ask all the questions I needed to understand the "why's" to everything. I even got to see intimate moments of how they handled setbacks, and oppositions privately vs. public facing. The positives went into the organization and the negatives stayed at the leadership level.

Now, as a business development professional, I acknowledge the magnitude of their mission, and I recognize the confidence they had in delivering the vision and engaging their congregation to take action. There was no room for marginal error. After all, their workforce and talent were all based on volunteers. It's wild to recount this event knowing they were a functioning piece of a movement that reached people's lives in major cities all over the world, all with a volunteer army. Now that's Strategy!

You see, there's good strategy, and then there's bad strategy. And believe it or not, both can look deceptively similar at first glance. But here's the catch, while they may share the same label, one of them lacks the vital components that propel a business in the right direction.

As an entrepreneur, identifying these characteristics early on will be the difference between penetrating the market and not. What differentiates a good strategy from a bad one? Here is the method I created, Formula ABC:

1. Analysis: Assessing the Approach

2. Blueprint: Building the Backbone

3. Consistency: Cultivating Cohesion

Remember Fred from chapter one, we talked about the intake and the initial conversation that took place to uncover his dilemma. This first step is crucial to understand that all problems are not the same and will not have the same approach.

Why is **Analysis** the cornerstone of effective strategy development? Because it involves a thorough examination and evaluation of the current state of any entrepreneur's business, it forces you to look at the internal and external factors that impact the development of your venture such as:

Internal

- Resources and Capabilities
- Team member roles
- Financial performance

External:

- Market trends
- Competitive landscape
- Economic Conditions
- Technology advancements

The Analysis stage is akin to discovering a precious vein of gold. Just like gold holds immense value, the insights and information gathered during analysis can be transformative and highly advantageous. However, it is important to remember that raw gold alone does not fulfill its potential. It must be refined and converted into a usable resource to truly reap its benefits.

Similarly, the knowledge gained through the Analysis phase of planning must be effectively translated into decisions that lead directly to action. This is in place to unlock the analysis's full potential and drive meaningful outcomes for your business. By uncovering a comprehensive analysis, you will not only unlock valuable insights into the ever-changing landscape of market dynamics, but you will get a better look at the competitive forces at play, customer behavior, and identify the capabilities of your own workflow. This meticulous assessment serves as a compass that will:

- guide you to uncover your hidden strengths

- acknowledge areas of improvement
- recognize promising opportunities
- navigate potential threats

Now that you're armed with this knowledge, you are empowered to make informed decisions that will pave the way for your successful journey ahead.

Going Back to Fred

After the analysis phases, my team got busy right away, so we designed a **Blueprint** for Fred. The blueprint, which is where we are Building the Backbone, serves as a guiding framework for the strategic plan to operate under. It encompasses the vision, goals, and objectives that drive the Entrepreneurs direction. What is the importance of the Blueprint? The blueprint provides:

- a structured plan that outlines the specific steps
- initiatives
- resources required to achieve strategic objectives

In essence the Blueprint phase is the process, specific steps and initiatives required to bring the strategy to life.

Case Study: From Vision to Chaos

Picture this: a multi-millionaire with a thriving career and successful second business decides to take on the challenge of owning not one, but two franchises within the membership industry. This journey would prove to be his greatest test yet.

As the story unfolds, you'll encounter two masters at odds: corporate and the franchisee. The national company's owners had a burning desire to replicate their personal networking club experience, fueled by a long list of grievances and an insatiable hunger for success. With dollar signs flashing before their eyes, they embarked on a mission to build the best in-person and virtual networking space, spanning every major city that would lead to eventually having a global presence.

However, amidst their grand vision, good strategic planning took a backseat and bad strategy prevailed. They made the critical mistake of assembling a top-heavy corporate team, armed with little industry experience beyond attending social club events. Driven by their belief in superior sales skills, impeccable alumni connections, and irresistible personalities, they wasted no time expanding to cities like DC, Miami, NY, Detroit, Chicago, Dallas, Philly, with Silicon Valley next on the horizon.

The franchise owner that reached out to me owned the DC franchise and was opening Silicon Valley soon. They required help with marketing, event hosting, and sales to boost membership for the Palo Alto site. The franchise owner insisted that I take on the DC site as well, he said it would be for a short period of time until he can get a project coordinator for that site. I reluctantly agreed, even though I had already built a plan for one site and didn't believe in spreading that time thin. Launching a site was going to take all the resources and energy.

I started my analysis process for the DC site, it didn't take long to identify the site was hemorrhaging money, had a small membership base, and lacked quality connections. The most alarming of them all was the fact that most of the memberships were given away at no cost.

Despite my proposals and solutions, there was little urgency to address the issues, with the shrinking resources and the opening of the new site in Palo Alto, DC was not top of mind.

Red Flag Alert

After two years in DC, they seemed content with the subpar conditions. The franchise owner's primary concern revolved around the exhaustion, time, and money already invested in the DC project, leading them to believe that the networking market in the area was simply not favorable. Their hopes and dreams now rested solely on the Silicon Valley site, convinced it would be a networking paradise. However, as I attended more corporate meetings on behalf of the franchise owner, it became evident that many decision-makers lacked the necessary expertise.

Budget discussions revealed unnecessary expenditure driven by the desire to outshine their previous boutique club, now their competition. The Corporate guys focus seemed fixated on showcasing their expansion into multiple cities and their independence. But the truth was far from their perceptions. The reality I witnessed during those meetings was a stark contrast to what they believed.

I spoke up in the meetings and had private conversations with the guys that owned corporate, but they ignored my suggestions, so I took matters into my own hands. I raised membership prices, introduced impactful events with influential speakers, and facilitated cross-migration between DC and Palo Alto. Members thrived, revenue began to turn around, becoming the top two franchises in sales volume, and connections led to increased business opportunities. Deal flow began to take place at the events that I was orchestrating. In those events I was the business match maker. When you take the time to get to know the community you're building, you gain an understanding of what it is that they need for their personal lives, family and business. The magic is when you can help them elevate it all.

Things were going well until corporate intervened, dismissing DC and Palo Alto's success. The owners rolled out strict rules stifling innovation. At the end of my term with the franchisee, I expressed my concerns to a sideline franchise owner about the company's trajectory and poor planning, but it fell on deaf ears. The sideline franchisee was blinded by the concept, not the strategy. Never, can a good concept compensate for a weak strategy, in this situation the success of Corporate and the Franchisees would require experienced individuals and a good strategy.

Not long after my departure, members reached out, sharing the company's downfall. The new franchise owner and corporate leadership became self-centered, banning members who voiced concerns which eventually led to its demise. Eventually, the owner realized their mistakes and approached me for not for help, but to offer my advice to redirect the disaster and revive the business. It was a validation not only of my initial observations, but of the strategies I shared with them back when I was aboard. I ultimately turned the conversation down but before we hung up with one another he posed the million-dollar question, "What would you do now, at this point?"

What do you think my response was?

1. Analysis: Assessing the Approach

2. Blueprint: Building the Backbone

3. Consistency: Cultivating Cohesion

In short, bad strategies and ego-driven decisions led to the company's decline.

You see, designing a good strategy is not just a mishmash of disjointed ideas and actions. No, it's a well-coordinated system of guiding frameworks and actions that work together seamlessly. It's like a symphony, where each instrument plays its part to create a harmonious wholesome performance.

It was a hard situation, with little to no autonomy and innovations. The franchise owner that I worked with, saw great potential in the concept, but the biggest barrier was the corporate guys and their ego.

Consistency in Cultivating Cohesion

Coherence involves identifying the relationships between different elements of the strategy and ensuring they work harmoniously together. It means avoiding contradictions or conflicting objectives that could lead to confusion or inefficiency. A coherent strategy not only eliminates discrepancies but also generates synergy, amplifying the impact of each individual component.

Consistent coherent action is like the final piece to the puzzle that brings the whole picture together. It emphasizes the importance of taking consistent and coordinated steps to implement the strategy effectively and aligning individual actions, decisions, and behaviors with the overall strategic direction. It requires clear communication, coordination, and a shared understanding among team members.

The natural by-product of coherent action extends beyond the strategy itself to foster communication and understanding among the team, ensuring that everyone, from leaders to employees, shares a common understanding of the strategic goals. Not only does this shared alignment mobilize resources and encourage collaborations, but it further instills a collective sense of purpose. When the entire team is in sync, they can effectively contribute to the overall strategy and work towards its success.

David and Goliath

In the book "Good Strategy/Bad Strategy," by Richard P. Rumelt he touches on the timeless tale of David and Goliath to illustrate the profound difference between good strategy and bad strategy. The story of David and Goliath is a perfect example of how perceiving and leveraging advantages can lead to remarkable outcomes, even in the face of seemingly insurmountable odds.

In the traditional narrative, Goliath, a towering and heavily armored giant, instilled fear, and intimidation in the hearts of his adversaries. The conventional wisdom was that defeating Goliath required an equally formidable opponent, someone who could match his size and strength. However, David, a young shepherd boy, saw the situation through a different lens.

David recognized that engaging Goliath in a toe-to-toe combat would be a grave loss. Instead, he reframed the situation and identified Goliath's weaknesses. Goliath's sheer size and armor made him slow and cumbersome, limiting his agility and maneuverability. David understood that exploiting these vulnerabilities would be the key to his victory.

Embracing a good strategy, David made a bold decision. He discarded the heavy armor and weapons typically used in battle and instead armed himself with his trusty slingshot. This choice surprised and worried those around him, as they couldn't comprehend how a simple slingshot could stand against the might of Goliath.

But David had a deeper understanding of the battlefield dynamics. He *analyzed* that by leveraging his agility, speed, and accuracy with the slingshot he had a *blueprint*, he could strike Goliath with precision before Goliath could even reach him. He aimed for the weak spot, Goliath's forehead, which was unprotected by his armor. David's strategy was not about matching Goliath's power head-on; it was about exploiting his vulnerabilities while capitalizing on his own strengths. *Coherent action* would bring it all together.

When the battle commenced, David's sling whirled, and a single stone flew towards Goliath. The stone found its mark, striking Goliath with such force that he fell to the ground, defeated. David's victory stunned both his allies and enemies. It was not the expected outcome, but it was the result of a well-executed strategy that focused on understanding and capitalizing on the true sources of advantage and weakness.

This story highlights the fundamental distinction between a good strategy and a bad one. A bad strategy would have dictated the conventional approach to match Goliath's power, that would have led to David's certain death. On the other hand, his approach to the situation required a clear understanding of circumstance, identification of key advantages and weaknesses, and a willingness to deviate from the norm. Trying to go at your business without the proper expertise or guidance would be to do what is expected, the norm. This is why most businesses fail within its first five years. Not because the product wasn't good, but because it was addressed in the same way everyone expects you to do your business, alone.

David's victory teaches us that a good strategy doesn't necessarily mean meeting the challenge head-on. It involves perceiving opportunities and leveraging unique strengths to create a path to success. Because he was able to reframe the situation by identifying the most critical factors, he was in turn, able to design a strategy that exploits them. As the legend goes David triumphed over Goliath, forever becoming a symbol of strategic thinking and courage in the face of overwhelming odds.

Listen up Entrepreneur

We need to share this same DNA when it comes to launching an idea and making it stick in the marketspace. Just like David, he only had one shot to knock Goliath down otherwise his element of surprise would no longer be a surprise.

As Entrepreneurs, we cannot afford to think like everyone else, that thinking would have gotten David killed with heavy weighted armor, putting him at a slow disadvantage trying to attack the giant head on.

Take Action

As an entrepreneur, what does your battlefield landscape look like? Can you easily analyze it?

Design a blueprint that identifies your advantage points and discards the unnecessaries.

Most importantly, once you analyze and design the blueprint, devise the actions that need to take place, serving as the cohesion.

https://bit.ly/-leading-with-purpose

Notes

Notes

[CH 4] Target Your N.I.C.H.E.

There is nothing more frustrating of a feeling than working with the wrong clientele. Imagine you are a luxury realtor, and you meet with a client, let's call this client "Adam", who informs you that he is in the market to buy a house. Adam produces his credit report that indicates he has excellent credit. Adam sends you a list of houses he saw online and would like to take a tour of these homes. You set up the appointments, and off you go, the house hunting begins. After three weeks of viewing homes and neighborhood research, he found the perfect luxury dream home. Now he begins the loan process, but a challenge occurs, the loan agent calls to inform you that even though Adam has great credit, he doesn't make enough money to qualify for the monthly installment payments.

Upon hearing this news, exhaustion immediately melts over you like a weighted moving blanket (pun intended), you think of all the time you invested into this buyer, only to discover he was never your target clientele.

You Now Have Two Options

a) Pivot your niche offer and price point outside of the luxury home market to cater to Adam's needs.

b) Refer Adam to a trusted colleague or real estate professional who specializes in non-luxury homes.

There are pros and cons to these options. While it may be tempting to adjust your business strategy to accommodate this particular client, it's important to assess whether this shift aligns with your long-term goals and brand positioning. You will consider the potential impact on your reputation as a luxury realtor and the value you bring to high-end clientele and way out your options.

On the flip side, by referring this client to an expert in a different market segment, you not only provide them with the best possible service but also strengthen your network and professional relationships. By referring Adam to a colleague demonstrates your commitment to the client's satisfaction and your willingness to prioritize their needs above all else. By making this referral, you maintain your integrity as a luxury realtor and ensure that your focus remains on serving your target clientele. This gesture can lead to future referrals and a positive reputation within the industry.

This is just an example; luxury realtors typically have a qualifying system in place before you meet with them. In most cases before you meet them you must be pre-qualified with a loan amount.

As a consultant most entrepreneurs that come to me have been in business for a couple of years and have hit a plateau. If the diagnosis is the wrong clientele, that is a hard pill to swallow. Just like the luxury realtor in this example, the entrepreneur recalls the amount of time they spent attracting the wrong audience, and thankfully the dots connect making sense as to why they have adjusted their product pricing so many times. Once they get over the initial blow, they do find comfort in knowing that there was nothing wrong with their product and their confidence begins to come back. Entrepreneurs are too close to the situation and need an outside audit and evaluation, someone that is not emotionally attached or biased to the time and effort that has been applied.

When it comes to identifying who your perfect clients are, use the method I created:

N. I. C. H. E., which targets each component of attracting your ideal consumer.

N-Narrow: Narrow down your target audience by identifying specific characteristics and demographics.

I-Identify: Identify the unique needs, desires, and pain points of your target audience.

C-Connect: Build a strong connection and rapport with your target audience through effective communication.

H-Highlight: Highlight the value and benefits your products or services offer to meet their specific needs.

E-Engage: Engage with your target audience through personalized interactions and tailored marketing strategies.

By understanding the components within N.I.C.H.E., you can effectively cater to your target audience, which in turn, positions you with healthy client retention.

Let's break it down...

N. I. C. H. E.

Narrow

Is to embrace the power of precision by identifying characteristics of who your ideal consumer is. You will want to stay away from casting a wide net, hoping to catch a few fish. Think of strategically narrowing down your target audience as a way to intentionally aim for the bullseye every time. In order to aim with precision, you must first identify the specific characteristics and demographics that align with your unique offering. This is the time to dig deep, to uncover the ideal consumer who will not only appreciate your value but will also become your brand's loyal advocates.

By narrowing this focus, you can amplify the impact by delivering tailored solutions that hit the mark EVERY TIME. You cannot afford to leave room for ambiguity or mediocrity. Becoming great lies in the details. When you don't have your audience down to a precise target it is the equivalent of gathering ducks and eagles and placing them in the same space. You will only frustrate the ducks and irritate the eagles; they just won't commingle or co-exist together. The wide targeted audience might want your product but cannot afford it or might not understand the value of needing it. Does this mean you change your product price, or do you change who your ideal client is?

This will soon become second nature to you, but you have to understand that connecting to your target audience will have to go beyond numbers and data points. It's about tapping into the realm of intuition, harnessing the power of empathy, diving into the mindset and emotions of your ideal consumer, speaking their language and anticipating their needs.

This intuitive approach allows us to craft messaging, products, and experiences that resonate on a deep level. It's all about building those authentic connections and forging relationships built on trust and mutual understanding. By embracing your intuitive nature, we can unlock the secret code to capture the hearts and minds of the desired target audience.

As entrepreneurs, we must aim for nothing less than compelling communication by creating a:

- Magnetic force that draws your target audience in
- Leaving them craving more
- Utilize the power of storytelling
- Using words and visualizations
- Weave narratives that captivate and inspire
- Lead with your brands voice

This will serve as the glue that will make your clients love your product so much that they will, on their own, tell as many people as possible about you. Decide on this compelling message that will be influential enough to cut through the noise, commanding their attention and igniting a genuine curiosity. Through compelling communication, you will leave a lasting impression, achieving optimal results when it comes to imprinting your brand in the minds of this consumer. Think of it as a way to infuse your ideal consumer at every touchpoint with the power of your compelling presence, which is positioning you as the brand authority in your industry. This will serve as a building block used to develop your empire that will stand the test of time.

Many entrepreneurs I talk with believe narrowing their focus is a limitation; but it's not, it will serve you as your superpower, creating a gravitational pull that attracts your ideal consumer straight to you. You cannot leave room for ambiguity or average. You have to consciously and continuously beat the average.

Narrowing down directly correlates to trusting your instincts and captivating the hearts and minds of your target audience. As you are reading this book now, think about the exact audience that raves about your product and gives glowing reviews about you. Identify them now and know them. By recognizing who that is, you will be able to start narrowing your aim to hit the bullseye. I personally only want to work with clients that believe in what I do, those who think my service and products are magical secret weapons that solve their problems. These are the types of clients I want for you too.

N. *I.* C. H. E.

Identify

To serve your ideal consumer we must go beyond surface-level demographics. You have to dive deep into the depths of their needs, desires, and pain points in order to identify their unique challenges they are up against. By doing this you are positioning yourself as the solution they've been searching for and so desperately need. There are many ways to do this, you can start by conducting thorough research, engaging in conversations, surveys, and market analysis to uncover the hidden gems of insight. Spoiler alert: This is not the time to guess or assume—this is the time to identify and conquer.

Earlier we talked about not settling for average. With that mentality in mind as entrepreneurs we strive for impact, and it starts with understanding our target audience on a profound level. By identifying their unique needs, desires, and pain points, you can align yourself with THEIR aspirations and struggles. You can develop a keen sense of empathy that will allow you to create offerings that make a real difference in their lives. Let's always be the entrepreneurs that don't just meet expectations; let's be the entrepreneurs that go above and beyond to exceed them. We become the catalyst for transformation, empowering our target audience to overcome obstacles and achieve their goals. We are the gold standard in our marketspace. Say it with me and say it out loud "I am the gold standard." Say it again, "I am the gold standard!"

In this crowded landscape of business, standing out will be essential for you. At Entrepreneurial Empire, we don't just blend in; we elevate our clients. As the entrepreneur who is reading this book, you too are the elevation to your consumer. So, by identifying the unique needs, desires, and pain points of your target audience, you will gain a competitive advantage that will push you into dominating your space. When you understand what sets you apart within your industry, you can use that knowledge to create experiences that will elevate your consumers' journey, with every stride you are exceeding their wildest expectations. Through elevating their experience, you become the brand they can't resist, their guiding light in a sea of mediocrity, propelling them towards success and helping them reach new heights.

N. I. *C.* H. E.

Connect

Entrepreneurs don't just aim to reach their target audience; they aim to forge a bond of brand authority. Building a strong connection starts with effective communication. We listen intently, absorbing every word and nuance. We engage in meaningful conversations, both online and offline, to truly understand their world. We speak their language, resonating with their hopes, dreams, and challenges. Through our authentic and genuine approach, we create a bridge of trust and rapport. We don't just communicate; we connect on a profound level.

Collaborating in the realm as an entrepreneurial empire, you have to believe that collaboration is key. Building a strong connection with our target audience means involving them in the journey. We value their input, ideas, and feedback. We embrace a co-creation mindset, working hand in hand to shape the solutions they truly need. Through collaborative efforts, we strengthen the bond and create a sense of ownership. We become partners in their success, leveraging their unique insights to fuel our growth. Together, we rise to new heights, united by a shared vision and unwavering commitment to excellence.

Entrepreneurs must be individuals who absolutely crush their market when it comes to going the extra mile. They must deliver exceptional value with every interaction. By applying the beat average concept, you leave no stone unturned in your quest to understand your ideal consumer's deepest needs and desires. The relationship to your consumer is that "we are in this together, conquering the challenges that come your way, transforming lives by becoming your solution."

In the realm of entrepreneurial empire, connecting with our target audience is not just a transactional experience; it's a transformational journey. If you have been struggling in your business with high turnover, assess your tone and demeanor. Does it translate to "we are here for you, as the solution to your needs, we got your back!" Do you handle your audience as a transaction with dollar signs in your eyes, or do you see opportunities where you can provide transformation and long-term impact by serving them.

When you are aligned with your ideal audience and your product matches your audiences' ultimate needs, you will feel like king Midas, known in Greek mythology, where everything he touched turned to gold. When you are operating in your highest potential, coupled with embracing your ideal customer, they will feel like you touched their situation with your product, and it turned their whole life around. MIDAS TOUCH! You will look at yourself in the mirror and say who is the lucky son of a gun that gets to meet me today, I am about to transform some lives with my business offer.

N. I. C. *H*. E.

Highlight

When you know the power of highlighting your product's value and benefits it will offer, you will see dramatic results in your consumers' buying behavior. As entrepreneurs our creed must be that we will meet our target audiences' specific needs and desires head on. We don't just deliver generic solutions; we tailor our offerings to address their pain points and aspirations. Through strategic messaging and compelling storytelling, we shine a spotlight on the unique value we bring to the table.

We go beyond the features and specifications. We dive deep into the transformational impact our products or services can have on their lives and businesses. We emphasize the outcomes, the results, and the tangible benefits they can expect. We paint a vivid picture of success and guide them towards the realization of their goals. Listen up entrepreneur, if you don't have a creed, borrow this one until you grow into your own.

Through captivating content, persuasive communication, and powerful testimonials, we ensure that our value proposition shines brightly, captivating our target audience and leaving a lasting impression.

But it doesn't stop there. Oh no, we keep it going, we don't just highlight the value; we amplify it. We showcase real-life examples, success stories, and case studies that demonstrate the tangible benefits our offerings bring. We let our track record speak for itself, illustrating the positive impact we've had on businesses just like theirs. Through thought leadership and educational resources, we empower our target audience with knowledge and insights that amplify their own potential for success. We become the beacon of expertise and authority, guiding them towards a brighter future.

Join us on this journey, where value is not just a concept but a reality that transforms businesses and propels them towards empire-building success.

N. I. C. H. *E.*

Engage

Entrepreneurs who are building empires understand that true connection and engagement are the keys to building a thriving community of loyal customers. We don't just preach about the importance of engagement; we live and breathe it in everything we do. We know that personalized interactions and tailored marketing strategies are the secret sauce to capturing the hearts and minds of our target audience.

We go beyond generic mass marketing approaches. We take the time to understand the unique preferences, interests, and communication preferences of our audience. We use this knowledge to create personalized experiences that resonate on a deep level. Through targeted messaging, customized offers, and one-on-one interactions, we establish a genuine connection that goes beyond transactions. We don't see dollar signs, we see people who need us, and we show up for them.

We believe in the power of listening and actively engaging with our audience. We encourage open dialogue, inviting feedback, and genuinely valuing our audiences' opinions. We create opportunities for participation, whether through surveys, contests, or interactive content, to foster a sense of belonging and ownership. By treating each interaction as an opportunity to build a lasting relationship, we cultivate a community of passionate supporters who champion our brand.

Engagement is not just a buzzword for us entrepreneurs; it's our way of life. We pride ourselves on going the extra mile to connect, communicate, and engage with our target audience. It's through these personalized interactions and tailored marketing strategies that we build an empire of loyal customers who not only believe in our brand but also actively contribute to its growth. If your mindset is to make money to pay the bills, then that is exactly what you will get. If your mindset is to create impact, then that is exactly what you will get. Decide what kind of entrepreneur you will be and become it.

Are you ready to unleash the power of N.I.C.H.E. and take your business to the next level? Here's your call to action:

I am expecting that you will:

- Narrow and Reflect: Take a moment to reflect on your current target audience and assess if it's narrowly defined. Are there specific characteristics and demographics you can identify to create a niche market?

- Identify: Dive deep into the unique needs, desires, and pain points of your target audience. Conduct market research, surveys, and engage in conversations to truly understand what drives them and how your offerings can address their specific challenges.

- Connect: Focus on building strong connections and fostering genuine relationships with your audience. Craft compelling messaging and communication strategies that resonate with them. Listen actively, respond authentically, and create a sense of community that keeps them engaged and loyal.

- Highlight: Showcase the value and benefits your products or services bring to your audience. Develop clear and compelling messaging that emphasizes the unique solutions you offer and the transformation you enable. Be relentless in communicating why your audience should choose you over competitors.

- Engage: Implement personalized interactions and tailored marketing strategies to actively engage with your audience. Use social media, email marketing, events, or other platforms to create personalized experiences and involve them in your brand story. Show them that you genuinely care about their success.

Now that you are armed with the power of N.I.C.H.E., take action and make quantum leaps towards building your entrepreneurial empire. Don't settle for mediocrity—strive for greatness, dominate your industry space of business, and leave a legacy.

Your empire awaits.

Take Action

Define who your target audience is by creating an avatar that represents your client. When you are designing your client avatar look for characteristics you want them to have. Ask yourself:

- Where do they shop?
- What are their values?
- Annual income?

Once you create your ideal customer persona, establish how your product addresses their challenges and enhances their daily lives.

By identifying your niche product list three clients that have already benefited from your offer and collect a video testimonial. You can place this on your website, social media, emails that highlight this product. This will begin to highlight the benefits of working with you and grab potential customers' attention.

Notes

Notes

[CH 5] Breakthrough in Pricing

In the world of entrepreneurship, there's a common struggle many of us face when it comes to pricing our products or services. It's a decision that can either hold us back or propel us towards success. As Rocky Balboa famously said, "If you know what you're worth, go out and get what you're worth. And not pointing fingers saying you're not where you want to be because of him or her." These powerful words serve as a reminder to recognize our own value and to stop settling for less than we deserve.

Entrepreneurs often fall into the trap of underpricing themselves, failing to fully appreciate their own brilliance and expertise. They may fear losing potential clients or believe that charging less will attract more customers. One might even find themselves in a drought and need a quick recovery. But in doing so, they undermine their own worth and limit their growth potential. It's time to let go of excuses and stop blaming others for our pricing decisions.

Unleashing our worth means having the confidence to set our price point based on the value we provide. It's about recognizing that our expertise, knowledge, and unique solutions are invaluable. When we embrace our worth, we attract clients who appreciate the transformative impact we can have on their lives and are willing to invest accordingly.

Case Study

I recently had a client, let's call her Nichole, she was incredibly brilliant when it came to business development. She knew the ins and outs of business and could help with any type of business no matter what phase they were in or what mess they found themselves facing. No matter where Nichole was, she could spill out strategy in networking meetups, over dinner, even in a bathroom stall. It came easy for her.

The problem was she recently went through a personal life transition, that caused her a serious setback. During this setback, she had to start from new and really hustle her way back to where she was. Along this journey up, she saw a need within the struggles she was facing and decided to pivot from her established niche clientele and began working with folks that were trying to turn their hustles into legit businesses. They were building a business on a shoestring budget and could barely afford to pay Nichole for her ridiculously dropped pricing rates. She took her pricing from $75,000 starting cost to $2,000 per client. She had a big heart with a big mission to help those just like her, that had to hustle, but she was killing herself doing it. When she came to me, she had explained the life setback, and her newly found passion to provide her expertise to the bootstrapper, shoestring budget entrepreneur.

I heard her out and understood the traumatic experience she went through. I shared with her my own personal experience with having to start over from nothing and the struggle to get the clients coming in. After digesting the information trying to connect the dots between her experience, expertise, and the clientele she was currently seeking, I had a problem doing so. Her connection to this clientele was not quite making sense for me. I pointed out that she was never really a shoestring budget bootstrapped business kind of entrepreneur. Here is exactly what I told her:

"You were in real estate in your early twenties and made great money, before you transitioned into consulting. You made even more money consulting before you went through a horrendous life setback. Honey, you were never a bootstrapper kind of gal. You had a level of experience that matches the billionaire clients that want your services in your arsenal. That is why it only took you a year to find yourself out of that, "left for broke" situation. Because you knew how! My question to you is why would you target an audience that is not mentally ready for your level of expertise?"

I immediately thought of the eagle and the duck scenario. Without asking, I could only imagine that the clientele she was working with was overwhelmed with the development planning she was offering to them, and I could imagine equally Nichole was frustrated as her clientele struggled with her directions. As our conversation progressed, she confirmed what I imagined. She explained the roadblocks that she was up against, but she was determined to get through and move past those challenges. The coaching that I provided was gentle but still a wake-up call level of coaching for her. I explained to Nichole that her brilliance is like speaking French to a person who only speaks Mandarin. Even if you try to physically show them what to do, there's such a large gap in the language barrier they won't understand what you're saying completely. She had an ah ha moment, and it immediately clicked. She was trying to make one million dollars with 500 clients per year at $2,000 per client. 500 clients was not realistic to her operation set up at all. Not when all she needed was 40 of her niche clients to purchase her $25k coaching package to make one million dollars. 40 clients vs. 500 clients was a wild variation.

As I continued to press in, I wanted to get a clear understanding of why this mission was so important to her for her to completely shift into a realm that was far from her perfectly paired audience. As we peeled back the layers and I asked more questions, bam, it happened, she was able to identify the very reason she set out on this mission, the underlying reason. Nichole was struggling with her confidence because she had lost everything. She didn't just lose financial status, and credibility, but she lost her confidence to face the kids in her sandbox. She never connected her experience as value, she only saw her bank account as her current value and status.

We got started right away on the mind shift. Society and social media says value comes in the form of followers and material things. When we really look at that skewed view on values, I can't help but point out, things do not create a person's worth of personal value. Once we got past that mind blockage, she never looked back, her wings were healed, and she soared like the eagle she always was.

Look, no matter what level an entrepreneur is at, stuff happens. That's why it's imperative to have the right mentors, coaches, and consultants in your corner.

People work with me because I am successful in transitioning them out of their funkary, be it personal or professional. I transcend them to the next level, wedging them out of plateau status.

If you are struggling with your pricing and you feel like you should be charging more, but you're afraid that you'll lose your audience, I'm going to let you in on a little secret... THEY'RE NOT YOUR AUDIENCE!

So, let's take Rocky's inspiring words to heart and embark on a journey to discover our true worth. It's time to cast aside limitations and doubts and step into our power. We have what it takes to create a thriving empire. It's time to stop settling for less and start pursuing what we truly deserve. By unleashing our worth and experiencing a breakthrough in our price point, we can transform our business and reach new heights of success.

When in doubt, evaluate P.R.I.C.E. - Powerfully Reap Impressive Coffers & Earnings

1. *Power Up Your Value*: Unleash the true power of your product by recognizing its unique value proposition. Identify the remarkable qualities, benefits, and solutions it brings to the table. Embrace your expertise and stand tall amidst the competition. Believe in the impact you can make and let that belief radiate through your pricing strategy.

2. *Roar with Confidence*: Price your product without fear or hesitation. Know your worth and refuse to settle for anything less. Stand firm in your convictions and convey an unshakeable confidence in the value you offer. Let your pricing

speak volumes about the caliber of your product and your unwavering commitment to excellence.

3. *Ignite Desire*: Set your pricing to evoke desire and ignite a burning passion in your target audience. Create a sense of urgency and exclusivity that makes them crave what you have to offer. Craft compelling pricing packages that capture their imagination, leaving them no choice but to say, "I must have it!"

4. *Command Premium*: Embrace the art of commanding a premium price for your exceptional product. Position yourself as the top-tier option in the market, the pinnacle of quality and innovation. Align your pricing with the unparalleled value you deliver, attracting customers who understand that greatness comes with a price.

5. *Elevate Your Empire*: Use pricing as a strategic tool to elevate your empire to new heights. Continuously evaluate and optimize your pricing strategy, keeping a keen eye on market dynamics and customer preferences. Adapt and evolve, always staying one step ahead, seizing opportunities to scale your business and conquer new territories.

With P.R.I.C.E., you possess the power to unlock the full potential of your product and propel your empire to unprecedented success. Embrace your power and let it shine through your pricing, paving the way for profitability, growth, and domination in your industry.

Take Action

Maybe you're in transition and you're determining pricing now. Look to the market and find what others are charging, identify what sets you apart from others, and decide what price aligns with your value and your service.

Reflect on a time that you offered your product at an undervalued price, how did it make you feel? Remember this feeling and decide now to evaluate your worth and your unique offer. When you set your price accordingly your target audience will show up.

Notes

Notes

[CH 6] Authentic Branding: Unicorn in the Marketspace

Aura is your distinctive atmosphere surrounding a given source. It is an energy field that is held to emanate from a living being.

Now that we have discussed your niche and price point, let's explore who you are as a brand in that coupled space. Where is your authenticity? What is your brand voice? Does your authenticity and brand identity go hand in hand?

As a business development professional, it's not just about the products or services we offer, but the genuine passion and enthusiasm we bring to the table. We believe that our authenticity and brand identity together are shaping our relationships and driving our success.

When it comes to selecting clients to work with, I stand firm in my beliefs. It's not about the size of the budget or the amount of money offered. What truly matters to me is aligning with entrepreneurs who have a strong mission and unwavering commitment to their vision. I want to work with individuals who are as passionate about their products as I am about making a difference in their businesses.

For me, it's personal. I dive deep into the projects, pouring my energy and expertise into every aspect. The greatest satisfaction comes from knowing that my efforts have made a tangible impact on my clients' clientele. It's not just about collecting a paycheck; it's about creating a positive ripple effect through businesses that genuinely matter.

Passion, I believe, is highly contagious, and I believe that when entrepreneurs lack that fire and enthusiasm, their business becomes a mundane checklist of tasks. I need to see that fire in their eyes when they talk about their business. I want to feel goosebumps when they express their excitement about their project. Is the belief in what they are doing seeping out of their pores. My style is a bit unorthodox; I can be wild, inventive, animated, and colorful. I am a creator; I bring visions to life. But because of this unorthodox approach, I will not work with the "I'm too cool entrepreneur," where image is more important than actual results. When I am in a room with this style entrepreneur, I can literally feel myself shrinking as if the oxygen in the room was being emptied. This style works for others, it's just not my sweet spot. If perception is more of a concern than coming from an authentic place, this will prevent their audience from getting to know them, which is not cohesive to building a culture of loyal brand advocates. At this juncture I can determine the project is too stiff for my unicorn magic and I will have to pass the work along. Working with clients that are open to their authentic version of themselves are the clients I take on.

In 2021 I was conducting a deep dive for a large audience of entrepreneurs; they came to this virtual event from all over North America tuning in to listen to our event keynote speaker Alan Olsen, managing partner at GROCO Advisors to the ultra-affluent and host of the famous podcast, "American Dreams." During this deep dive Alan made a point that struck out at me, it suddenly made sense of my belief in entrepreneurship. He said, "understand who you are and what your strengths are." He asked, "What are you good at? Decide what needs in the world you can solve with your unique capabilities."

Instantly I knew that's why I was drawn to entrepreneurhood. I never started out in my career thinking how much money I could make, or how well known I could become. I started my journey because I saw a need, a frustration and a complaint in the market space and connected those dots. The connection spoke out to me, calling my name. I had a talent within a certain skill set, and I became the solution to that specific problem. Up until this point, I had worked on many projects with all types of businesses, non-profit organizations, government agencies and startups. I was good at a lot of things when it came down to business development, narrowing down my niche helped my focus but when I heard Alan's message, I downshifted gears once again. What I understood was that my aura is my superpower. Once I realized this, it completely changed the clients that I took on.

A.U.R.A.

When I began to break down the meaning of A.U.R.A. I developed the four pillars Authenticity Uniqueness Reliability Appeal.

Authenticity refers to the genuine and true nature of your brand. It's about staying true to your values, beliefs, and mission. Authenticity doesn't chase money or clients, no, it is the reason clients chase you and money follows. Being authentic means being transparent and honest in your interactions with your audience. Allowing your audience to get to know the real you and be on this journey with you. It's about showing up as your true authentic self, without pretending to be someone you're not. Authenticity will build trust and foster meaningful connections between you and your customers, as they can relate to you and resonate with your genuine brand persona. Think about it like growing your circle of friends, you wouldn't hang out with someone that you couldn't relate to or love being around, it wouldn't be a prosperous relationship otherwise. That is the same for your customers; ask yourself, are your customers getting the real you? Your customers should be attracted to you because you align with their values and mission in life. Find that and you have found your community of followers and ambassadors.

Uniqueness is about standing out from the crowd and offering something distinct and different in the market. It's about identifying and highlighting your unique selling propositions (USPs) that set you apart from your competitors. Embrace your strengths, expertise, and innovative ideas to create a one-of-a-kind brand identity. Learning your uniqueness will not only help you capture the attention of your target audience but will make them recognize and remember your brand among the sea of competitors. This is like your fingerprint, there is not one person on this planet that will have an identical fingerprint as you. I'm sure you've heard the saying, "we are all born an original but many of us will die as a duplicate." Meaning, there's too many people trying to do the same thing with the same ingredients. Be unique, stand out, as scary as it might be, try something different but something that's you.

In my client relationships, I often receive heartfelt feedback from them expressing how much they enjoy working with me. They describe the experience as feeling like home, where they are embraced like family and truly valued. Clients feel comfortable enough to let their guard down and be their authentic selves, knowing they are in a safe and supportive environment. This sense of belonging and trust creates a unique bond that goes beyond the typical consultant-client relationship.

When it comes to the projects we collaborate on, clients are thrilled with the way I bring their visions to life. They commend my ability to perform at a consistently high level, ensuring that every aspect of the project is executed with excellence. Whether it's through meticulous attention to detail, innovative problem-solving, or going the extra mile to exceed expectations, I am dedicated to delivering exceptional results. This is what makes me unique aside from my actual skill set for the work itself. Take a snapshot of your uniqueness and determine what makes you unique in your career or as a business owner with your product offer. What are your customers saying about you?

Reliability encompasses the consistency and dependability of your brand. It means delivering on your promises and consistently meeting or exceeding customer expectations. This is what will build trust and foster that long-term customer loyalty. By consistently providing high-quality products or services, exceptional customer service, and reliable support, you establish a reputation as a reliable and trustworthy brand that customers can rely on. What is your gold standard of reliability, what can your customers depend on you for? Reliability will also tie into pricing, if you are charging too little, you will begin to feel overwhelmed and as though you're working for free. This can affect your consistency and reliability. In this category, you will want to make sure that two plus two equals four.

Earlier on in my career, I took on a client and didn't evaluate the steps involved properly, which caused me to put in more time and personal money to deliver the impact I envisioned for them. By the time I was done with the project, it was my best work up to that point, the client was so happy with the results. However, it cost me the entire price of the project plus five hundred dollars out of my own pocket to deliver on time and with great quality. Essentially working for free. I understood that I was not willing to jeopardize my brand reliability because I misjudged the project budget. Industry colleagues advised me to inform the client and ask for an expanded budget, but I couldn't. I evaluated the situation and concluded that by asking for a bigger budget because I failed to calculate the project's bandwidth did not align with my brand authenticity, uniqueness, reliability, or my appeal. Therefore, I could not follow that advice and thankfully I didn't, because that project led to others. Don't worry, I made sure to price it correctly after this experience.

Appeal refers to the attractiveness and allure of your brand to your target audience. It involves creating a visually appealing brand identity, including your logo, colors, typography, and overall design aesthetics. Additionally, appeal extends beyond the visual aspects and includes crafting compelling messaging and storytelling that resonates with your audience's emotions and aspirations. Your brand should evoke positive emotions, making your audience feel connected and drawn to your offerings. Again, taking this back to growing your inner circle of friends, you probably know exactly how your friends think, what they like and don't like, how they talk and what to get them for their birthday. When you treat your customers like your close circle of friends you will know how to appeal to their needs.

Take Action

1. Authenticity Audit: Ask yourself the following questions:

   - Am I being transparent and honest in my interactions with my audience?

   - Does my brand stay true to its values, beliefs, and mission?

2. Uniqueness Exploration: Understand what sets your brand apart from the competition. Consider the following:

    - What are your unique selling propositions (USPs)?

    - How can you embrace your strengths, expertise, and innovative ideas to create a one-of-a-kind brand identity?

    - How can you communicate your uniqueness effectively to your target audience?

3. Reliability Assessment: Evaluate your brand's reliability and commitment to delivering exceptional results. Ask yourself:

    - Are you consistently meeting or exceeding customer expectations?

    - How can you improve your reliability and establish a trustworthy reputation?

4. Appeal Enhancement: Review your brand's visual identity and messaging to ensure they are appealing to your target audience. Consider: Is your logo, colors, typography, and overall design aligned with your brand's personality and values?

    - How can you craft compelling messaging and storytelling that resonates with your audience's emotions and aspirations?

    - Are you evoking positive emotions and creating a sense of connection with your customers?

Take this time to complete these exercises and reflect on the results. Identify areas for improvement and develop an action plan to enhance your authenticity, uniqueness, reliability, and appeal. Remember, these pillars are the foundation of your brand's success and can help you create a loyal community of followers and brand advocates.

https://bit.ly/-AURA

Notes

Notes

[CH 7] Beyond Illusions: Embracing the Grit and Setbacks of Entrepreneurhood

Entrepreneuring is about taking action. It's easy to dress like an entrepreneur, buy a car like an entrepreneur, and even buy a big house like one. It's easy to look at an entrepreneur and fantasize over their lifestyle and the things they have or the way they're living their life, but what isn't fantasized widely is the struggle, the challenges, mindset and the setbacks.

When an entrepreneur is on the rise, it's common to see individuals fixated on the allure of fame and fortune, while completely overlooking the essential steps that lay the firm foundation for true success. What most people don't see is the grind, the long hours of hard work, the countless "No's", the inevitable losses, and failures along the way that build character. It's easy to get swept away with what they see once an entrepreneur has made it through the jungle of uncharted territories and overlook the bangs and bruises they acquired through that journey. It's often in hindsight that many failed entrepreneurs come to realize they didn't properly evaluate or analyze their situation or their game plan. Instead of building their blueprint to weather the market, they built their plan to acquire a luxury lifestyle. They misread the handbook on success and skipped a very crucial and critical ingredient.

The building of resilience and the lessons learned through failure are what will become your best friend that stretches your critical thinking muscle, that will eventually lead you to success. We're talking about real actual success.

I have encountered entrepreneurs who faced a difficult dilemma on whether to keep their businesses afloat or shut them down because they had adopted a lavish lifestyle before actually earning success. In those conversations, they were in need of a convincing "cover story" for closing their business, yet they did not hesitate to maintain an expensive luxury car payment, merely to save face. They had been advised by others to "fake it till you make it," but what they weren't warned about was the inevitable reality that would eventually catch up with them. Their high living expenses created a financial burden, preventing them from allocating resources for essential business operations and growth. Unfortunately, the facade tends to crumble at the most inopportune times.

Lesson Learned

About six years ago I left a relationship with absolutely nothing, and when I say nothing, I mean nothing, not a car, or a penny to my name and five kids to support. At one point in that relationship money was never an issue, we had six cars, two houses and we were also business partners. The decision to end a relationship that had a lot on the line, kids involved and all the other factors, was one of the hardest decisions I ever had to make. I was a mom of five kids, ages 2 - 17 years old. We were living in Silicon Valley, one of the most expensive places to live on planet earth. I held fast to the reality of the situation, and focused on the fact that I would be leaving a situation with nothing and no access to money, that was beyond scary. How would I support my family immediately, where do I even start?

During that time, right before the split, I experienced extreme panic attacks that would send me to the hospital on numerous occasions. My heart would beat so hard, dizziness would take over and I would fall to the floor. This decision was overwhelming, but I knew it had to be done. As I think about that time in my life it reminds me of the scene from the Titanic, starring Leonardo DiCaprio, where the entire ship is lifted in the air and it's about to go completely under. The fear gripping the characters in this scene, they were about to face this horrible thing and there was nothing they could do to change it, the only action they could take was to decide what they would do once they hit the water. DiCaprio explains that they were going to have to "fight like hell" to swim up as soon as the boat goes under, otherwise the pull of the ship will drown them, and further instructs them to take a deep breath right before entering the water. This decision was going to either drown me or I was going to have to fight like hell to get to the surface. Getting to the surface was just the beginning, I would still have to rebuild my life and plan my children's new future, that was going to take all my focus and all my energy.

Gone were the days of luxury and abundance. Everyone knew my lifestyle, so as you can imagine, it was the most humbling experience for me to have nothing and face everyone around me. Naturally, I didn't want people to know about my failed marriage or penniless status, but I had to let that mentality go. I struggled with the decision to reveal my situation, and become vulnerable to others. My imagination ran wild at times, I would imagine people feeling happy for my misfortune, and others feeling sorry for me. Throughout the reel of what I imagined, none of it was positive, but I knew I couldn't go on living in hiding.

To my surprise, the moment I let that concealment go, and told the world where I was at in life, a sense of liberation washed over me, granting me the freedom to acknowledge my circumstances and embrace the truth. Rather than pretending that everything remained unchanged, I discovered the strength in accepting my reality. There was power in owning my reality and from there, I was able to design a truly authentic path to climb out of that situation. Facing this reality gave me more than liberation, it gave me personal power, I could now stand confidently up against humiliation and popular vote.

In the beginning, I didn't know how to align my expertise as an accomplished entrepreneur who was seasoned with experience, side by side to my new situation of having nothing. Talk about a mindset whirlwind. Mentally I was challenged everyday with the temptation to associate and compare my newly found income status to my long standing expertise in business development. On days that I couldn't see past my current state I would conclude that I had no value. But that simply wasn't true, thankfully I had people surrounding me that spoke life into me like my dad, my Aunt Mela, and my two older kids Gilbert and Victoria.

Aside from this setback the more pressing issue was that I had no money and I had five kids to support financially and emotionally. I needed money and I needed it fast. I had to redefine my identity as an entrepreneur and refuse to let my circumstances define me. Due to my skills and knowledge, I leaned into the essence of entrepreneurhood like never before.

During that period, I witnessed entrepreneurs who failed to embrace the mindset of lifelong learning and mastery of their skillset. As a result, they lacked the essential abilities needed to navigate the challenges and uncertainties that came with the journey, they did not possess the skills necessary to survive and weather the storms of entrepreneurial life. They felt wedged into a corner where their only option was to give up instead of pressing through. When the storm approaches, the road ahead becomes dim, then it becomes dark, and if your skills are not up to par, you don't dare to keep stepping into the unknown.

Alone with my thoughts, I could have easily talked myself into throwing in the towel, and trust me, no one would have blamed me. With the pressure my family and friends saw me under it was painful for them to watch. It was similar to watching a boxer that is getting the living daylights beat out of them and every time they get knocked down to the floor, they keep rising to their feet. If you've ever watched a fight like this, you see the shift in the audience's demeanor and tone. If people were not cheering for that particular boxer to begin with, at first, they're happy to see him lose, but then the shift happens right about the time when the fight isn't just physical anymore, it becomes mental. As this boxer is getting the beating of his life, the audience now attaches themselves to him because he preserves, refusing to stay down, he doesn't give up, he's not a quitter. The audience witnesses real courage, triggering a sense of hope and fight for themselves on a deeper personal level. At this point, even if the boxer doesn't win, he still becomes the victor in everyone's mind. He championed through and stuck it out.

In part I knew I had the skills to make my own money as an entrepreneur, but I knew I had to believe in myself if I was going to make it to the 12th round of this bout. I can say I am so glad I became a student first, then the lifestyle came after in my first go at entrepreneurship. Because of my dedication to learning the skills for many years prior to losing everything, I was able to survive the 12th round on my feet. Growing up I remember hearing people throw around the saying "God will only give you what he knows you can handle." During these times I would ponder on that and think, wow God is strengthening for something even bigger down the road. As I persevered, I realized that my story was far from over. I held on to the belief that if God trusted me with this journey, then He had something extraordinary in store for me.

My faith in God is what carried me through and still is what carries me through now. My significant other told me recently that I am cursed with blessings, your blessings just keep coming and they are getting bigger and bigger. When you go through the hardest parts of entrepreneurship the only place you can run to is prayer. My faith did not retreat, it expanded. The resilience that is forged through the flames of opposition and challenges has made me bulletproof. My feet are planted on solid ground. When I face challenges today, I'm not scared or doubtful, I embrace it.

Listen up Entrepreneur

Reflect upon your journey and ask yourself:

- What kind of entrepreneur am I today?

- Am I continuously seeking opportunities to improve myself?

- Am I a genuine article, relentlessly dedicated to honing my skills and talents?

- Do I actively seek out those who have walked the path before me?

- Am I the type that merely pretends to be successful until I achieve it, driven by the allure of having a fancy title?

- Do I make it a daily ritual to absorb others' wisdom, learning from their mistakes and their triumphs?

It's time to elevate your mindset and commitment to excellence. Embrace the path of a true entrepreneur—one who passionately pursues knowledge and is unafraid to challenge themselves. Surround yourself with mentors and role models who inspire and guide you, taking in their invaluable insights. By adopting this mindset, you unlock the key to accelerated growth and surpassing your goals. It's not about faking it; it's about becoming an unstoppable force of knowledge, experience, and genuine success. Embrace the journey of continuous learning and empower yourself to reach new heights.

My belief in entrepreneurhood correlates to the parable of the talents in Matthew 25:14-30. The parable highlights a leader who was leaving town, and upon leaving he gathered his three entrusted stewards to take responsibility for his assets while he was away on travel. The assets were assigned to each steward according to their capabilities. The first steward received five talents, the second received two talents and the third steward received one talent. After some time had passed, the leader returned. The leader requested an account of his assets while he was away from each of his stewards. The first and the second steward described their efforts and recounted their ability to multiply the talents by double. Naturally the leader was pleased, he invested in them, trusted them to do better and they did. When it came to the third steward, he presented to the leader the same asset with no growth. He was given one talent and he returned one talent. The steward immediately explained his position, he told the leader that he didn't want to risk losing the one talent by making the wrong decision with it, so he kept it safe by storing it. When the leader heard this, he was not only disappointed, but upset. He ordered the one talent to be given to the steward with the ten talents and removed the steward from the place of business, casting him away. The leader stated, "to those who are given, will have abundance and to those who have not will always be in the negative." This parable has been my north star. We are all given talents and abilities, strengths that are unique that we have been entrusted with. We are either honing those skills and multiplying them or we are hiding them away, afraid to take a chance on ourselves. This parable served as my compass, whenever I felt like quitting, it would always point me north. Anything less than giving my all would just not suffice.

Take Action

Reflect on your entrepreneurial journey and answer the following questions:

What kind of entrepreneur am I today?

- Am I continuously seeking opportunities to improve myself?

- Am I genuinely dedicated to honing my skills and talents?

- Do I actively seek out those who have walked the path before me?

- Do I make it a daily ritual to absorb others' wisdom, learning from their mistakes and triumphs?

Write down the importance of embracing a mindset of continuous learning and commitment to excellence as an entrepreneur. Discuss how surrounding yourself with mentors and role models can contribute to your growth and success.

- Research and find a successful entrepreneur who has openly shared their struggles, setbacks, and lessons learned. Reflect on the key lessons you can apply to your own entrepreneurial journey.

- Read the parable of the talents in Matthew 25:14-30. Write a personal reflection on how this parable relates to your entrepreneurial mindset and approach to utilizing your talents and abilities. Discuss the significance of taking risks, embracing growth, and not settling for mediocrity.

- Choose one specific area of your entrepreneurial skill set that you want to improve. Create a plan outlining the steps you will take to enhance your knowledge and expertise in that area. Set measurable goals and a timeline for achieving them.

Let us regularly review our progress and adjust as necessary. You are the captain of this ship, stir it in the direction that leads to your desired destination. As entrepreneurs, we must recognize that the journey is not a straight path, but rather a dynamic and ever-changing voyage. It is our responsibility to stay vigilant and adaptable, keeping a keen eye on our goals while navigating through the unpredictable waters of entrepreneurship.

Remember, as the captain of your ship, embrace a mindset of agility, resilience, and constant self-improvement. Embrace the winds of change, embrace the unknown, and be ready to adjust your sails accordingly.

Notes

Notes

[CH 8] Paving the Path to Scaling Success

As an entrepreneur, the journey of scaling your business is an exhilarating endeavor that requires careful navigation. It demands a deep understanding of your unique vision, a keen sense of adaptability, and a commitment to continuous improvement. In this chapter, we will explore the essential strategies to consider as you embark on the path to scaling, tailored to your own style and aspirations.

The first question that should cross your mind is, when is the right time to scale? Let's consider a few signs that indicate it may be time to consider scaling:

1. Consistency in Demand indicates that there is an opportunity to expand and capture a larger share of the market.

2. Capacity Constraints: If you're consistently operating at or near maximum capacity and struggling to keep up with customer demand, it may be time to expand your operations.

3. Financial Stability: Scaling requires investments in resources, marketing, infrastructure, and talent, so ensuring that your business has a solid financial foundation is crucial.

4. Competitive Landscape: Staying ahead of the competition often requires expanding your operations, improving your offerings, or reaching new customer segments.

While these signs can indicate that it's time to scale, it's important to conduct a thorough analysis of your business, market conditions, and resources before making any decisions. Develop a well-defined scaling strategy, assess the potential risks and challenges, and ensure that you have the necessary resources, capabilities, and support to execute your scaling plans effectively.

Now that we took a look at a few signs that can indicate it is time to scale, let's look at one of the key pillars of crafting a scalable business model. This requires careful attention to building a solid foundation that will support the weight of expansion and ensure sustainable growth in the long run. By focusing on foundational excellence, you can set yourself up for success and navigate the challenges that come with scaling. In Chapter 1 we covered laying the foundation, but when you consider scaling your business into that equation you will want to start with the end in mind. Here are some essential steps to consider when crafting a scalable business model:

- Develop a Model by the consideration of implementing scalable processes and systems that can accommodate increased demand without sacrificing quality. Automate repetitive tasks, invest in technology solutions, and develop efficient workflows to improve productivity and scalability. Basically, you're looking for ways to provide reliability through automation and residual processes. This will cost you upfront, but it will be well worth the investment long-term.

Let's take a closer look at your operations, processes, and workflows to identify areas that can be streamlined and optimized to eliminate inefficiencies. By streamlining your operations, you can free up resources and ensure that your business is operating at its optimal level.

Remember, scaling is not just about expanding your business; it's about doing so in a way that ensures long-term success and maintains the quality and value to your customers' expectations.

Case Study

McDonald's and the Scaling of the Fast-Food Industry

One of the most iconic examples of scaling in the business world is McDonald's, the global fast-food giant. Founded in 1940 by Richard and Maurice McDonald as a small barbecue restaurant in San Bernardino, California, McDonald's underwent a transformative journey that propelled it to become one of the largest and most recognizable brands in the world.

In the early years, McDonald's faced the challenges that many small businesses encountered at the time. However, their approach to scaling the business set them apart. They introduced the "Speedee Service System," which focused on streamlining operations and providing fast, efficient service. This system laid the foundation for McDonald's ability to scale rapidly and consistently deliver their signature product: hamburgers.

In 1955, Ray Kroc, a skilled entrepreneur, recognized the potential of McDonald's and acquired the company from the McDonald brothers. Kroc's vision was to turn the restaurant into a franchise model, allowing for expansion on a much larger scale. He introduced standardized operating procedures, efficient kitchen layouts, and strict quality control measures to ensure consistency across all McDonald's locations.

The key to McDonald's success in scaling was its relentless focus on efficiency and replicability. By developing standardized processes and systems, they could maintain the quality and taste of their food, regardless of location. This allowed them to rapidly expand the number of restaurants and reach a broader customer base.

Another critical factor in McDonald's scaling journey was its strategic partnerships. In the early 1960s, the company partnered with suppliers to ensure a consistent and reliable supply chain. By forging alliances with trusted partners, McDonald's was able to scale without compromising on the quality of their ingredients or menu offerings.

Furthermore, McDonald's leveraged the power of franchising as a growth strategy. Franchising enabled individuals to invest in and operate their own McDonald's restaurants, spreading the brand's reach even further. The franchise model not only accelerated expansion but also distributed the risk and financial burden of scaling.

As McDonald's continued to scale, it adapted its menu and marketing to cater to different regional preferences and cultural nuances. This localization strategy allowed them to resonate with diverse markets worldwide while maintaining the core McDonald's experience. By understanding the importance of adapting to local tastes and preferences, McDonald's was able to successfully navigate cultural differences and establish a global empire.

Today, McDonald's operates in over 100 countries and serves millions of customers daily. Its success in scaling can be attributed to its ability to maintain operational efficiency, forge strategic partnerships, embrace franchising, and adapt to diverse markets. McDonald's exemplifies how a company can leverage scaling strategies to build an empire and become a dominant player in the fast-food industry.

Crafting a Scalable Model

The next step to creating a scalable business model is to expand your market reach to unlock untapped growth potential. Venturing into new markets and reaching a broader customer base opens up a whole new world of opportunities for your business. Here are key components to consider when expanding your market reach:

- Before entering new markets, you will want to conduct comprehensive market research to gain a deeper understanding of the market landscape, customer demographics, buying behaviors, and competition. Identify untapped opportunities and high-growth segments that align with your business offerings and capabilities. This research will serve as a foundation for developing an effective market expansion strategy.

- Develop a robust marketing strategy that will successfully expand your market reach. This plan should encompass various channels and tactics to reach your target audience effectively such as: digital marketing, social media platforms, content marketing, search engine optimization (SEO), and pay-per-click (PPC) advertising. With this type of marketing, you can tailor your messaging and positioning to resonate with the specific needs and preferences of your expanded audience.

- Digital Channels are essential for market expansion. Establish a strong online presence through a well-designed website that is optimized for search engines and user experience. Utilize social media platforms to engage with your target audience, build brand awareness, and drive traffic to your website. The content within these various platforms must include videos that highlight what you do, along with video testimonials. We live in a digital content world where seeing is believing. People want to get to know you before they dive into a commitment to you. The more videos you can provide the better. You will definitely want to create valuable blog posts, exciting videos, and downloadable resources to attract and educate your potential customers.

Now that we are looking into ways to grow our customer audience it is important to consider that scaling your business requires more than just a one-person effort. It requires a high-performing team that shares your vision, drives growth, and delivers exceptional results. Here are key strategies for cultivating a high-performing team that can thrive in the scaling journey:

- **Look for candidates** who not only possess the necessary skills and qualifications but also share your passion and enthusiasm for the business.

- **Empower your team through training and staff development** that will enhance their capabilities, by investing in their professional development opportunities. Offer ongoing learning initiatives, mentorship programs, and workshops to nurture their growth and unlock their full potential. This will serve as the retaining factor in keeping good talent.

- **Foster a culture of collaboration** that encourages teamwork, open communication, and cross-functional collaborations. Break down silos and create opportunities for employees to collaborate on projects, share ideas, and leverage their diverse skill sets. Encourage a supportive and inclusive environment where everyone feels valued and empowered to contribute.

- **Encouraging Innovation and Risk-Taking** by encouraging your team to think creatively, challenge the status quo, and take calculated risks that are embraced failure is seen as a stepping stone to learning and improvement. Provide the necessary resources and support for innovative initiatives and recognize and reward employees for their contributions.

- **Promote Continuous Improvement** by encouraging your team to seek feedback, learn from their mistakes, and embrace a growth mindset. Regularly evaluate processes, workflows, and strategies to identify areas for improvement and implement changes accordingly.

- **Recognize and Reward Performance** to motivate and inspire your team. Implement a performance management system that acknowledges and celebrates achievements, both as an individual and on a team basis. This can be done by offering incentives, bonuses, promotions, and other forms of recognition to show appreciation for their hard work and dedication.

By cultivating a high-performance team that aligns with your vision, values, and goals, you are creating a solid foundation for scaling your business. Invest in their growth and development, foster a culture of collaboration and innovation, promote continuous improvement, and recognize and reward exceptional performance. With a motivated and empowered team, you can drive growth together, overcome challenges, and achieve your scaling objectives.

Finally, prioritizing customer experience and retention is essential for sustainable growth. By delivering exceptional experiences, personalizing offerings, and implementing customer retention strategies, you can build loyalty, nurture relationships, and foster long-term customer loyalty.

A scalable model comes in all shapes and sizes, consider that you are a business coach and the next step to your business plan is to sell licensee rights to other coaches to utilize your material and train it to others for a fee. By doing this, you have widened your audience past the regular clientele you would normally attract with your service, but now you can offer your program to businesses with a training and staff development department and to coaches that are just starting their careers, who need a good foundational program to offer.

Another scenario is let's say you're an independent loan agent, you can recruit other agents that you bring into the industry, develop a training program that guides their success and charge a small percentage. Your audience just widened from potential home buyers to other agents who want to learn from you.

Take Action

The opportunity to scale your business is endless when you're growing an empire. Know your options and be aware of the budget.

1. Reflect on Your Current Business Model:

   - Evaluate your current business model and identify areas that can be streamlined and optimized for scalability.

   - Make a list of processes and systems that can be automated or improved to accommodate increased demand without compromising quality.

   - Research and identify technology solutions that can enhance productivity and scalability in your specific industry.

2. Conduct Market Research:

- Choose a specific target market or segment that you would like to expand into or reach.

- Conduct comprehensive market research to identify untapped opportunities and growth potential within that market.

- Develop a market analysis report that includes key insights, customer demographics, competitors, and potential challenges.

3. Create a Marketing Strategy:

- Develop a comprehensive marketing strategy that encompasses digital channels, social media, content marketing, and targeted advertising campaigns.

- Tailor your messaging and content to resonate with your expanded audience.

- Outline specific marketing tactics and channels you will utilize to reach your target market.

4. Assess Your Team and Hiring Needs:

- Evaluate your current team and identify any gaps or areas where additional talent is needed for scaling.

- Develop a hiring plan and criteria for new team members who align with your company's vision, values, and possess the necessary skills for supporting your expansion plans.

- Create a professional development plan to empower your existing team members and enhance their capabilities.

5. Research Strategic Partnerships:

    - Identify potential strategic partners in your industry who can help accelerate your scaling efforts.

    - Research and analyze their networks, distribution channels, and technology platforms to determine how they align with your business goals.

    - Develop a list of potential partnership opportunities and outline the mutual benefits that can be gained from collaboration.

6. Develop a Customer Experience and Retention Strategy:

    - Analyze your current customer experience and retention efforts and identify areas for improvement.

    - Create a plan to personalize your offerings, listen to customer feedback, and proactively address their needs and pain points.

    - Outline customer retention strategies such as loyalty programs, targeted marketing campaigns, and regular communication to nurture relationships and foster long-term customer loyalty.

7. Reflect on Your Scaling Journey:

    - Write a reflection on your current understanding of scaling and how the

> strategies outlined in this chapter align with your business goals.

- Identify any challenges or concerns you anticipate facing during the scaling process and brainstorm potential solutions.

8. Set specific goals and milestones for your scaling journey and develop a plan to track your progress and measure success.

Notes

Notes

[CH 9] Partnerships Built to Last

Let's talk about the power of partnerships and how they can contribute to the lasting success of your business. In today's interconnected and collaborative business landscape, forming strategic alliances is crucial for growth and sustainability. This requires the knowledge of key principles and strategies that layer the foundation on building partnerships that stand the test of time.

There is great value in synergy, when you're looking into forming the most successful partnerships they will have obvious commonalities that will be built on shared values, complementary strengths, and a mutual understanding of goals. Partnerships are not formed overnight, so taking your time is worth the exploration of identifying and evaluating all potential partners who align with your vision and mission. By harnessing the power of synergy, you can combine forces to achieve common objectives, amplify your reach, and enhance the value you offer to customers.

Synergy is the magical ingredient that fuels the success of partnerships. It goes beyond the sum of individual efforts and creates a dynamic where the collective output is greater than the sum of its parts. When partners come together, bringing their unique strengths, expertise, and resources, they have the potential to achieve remarkable results that would be challenging to attain independently as solopreneurs.

The value of synergy lies in the ability to tap into diverse perspectives and skill sets. Each partner brings a different set of experiences, knowledge, and capabilities to the table. By leveraging these differences, synergistic partnerships can solve complex problems, innovate, and create unique offerings that stand out in the market.

Synergy also fuels growth and expansion. When partners align their goals and work collaboratively, they can combine resources, networks, and market access to reach new heights. By pooling their strengths, they can access larger markets, penetrate new segments, and explore opportunities that would be out of reach individually. This collective power allows for accelerated growth and the potential to scale operations.

Case Study: The Synergy of Partnership- Steve Jobs and Apple

In the annals of entrepreneurial history, few stories are as legendary as that of Steve Jobs and Apple Inc. He is hailed as the visionary genius behind Apple's success, which anyone could acknowledge was indeed a driving force. However, it is crucial to recognize that Jobs did not embark on this revolutionary journey alone. From the very beginning, he understood the power of partnerships and the impact they could have on shaping the future of Apple.

When Steve Jobs co-founded Apple in 1976, he joined forces with Steve Wozniak, a brilliant engineer and programmer. Together, they complemented each other's skills, with Jobs focusing on the business side and Wozniak channeling his technical expertise. This partnership was the cornerstone of Apple's early success.

The partnership doesn't end there, as Apple grew, so did the collaborative partnerships. An example of this was his collaboration with industrial designer Jonathan Ive. With Ive's remarkable design sensibilities and Jobs' unwavering commitment to simplicity and elegance, they forged a creative bond that led to groundbreaking products like the iMac, iPod, and iPhone. This partnership not only elevated Apple's brand but also revolutionized the way we interact with technology.

Jobs further understood that strategic alliances could accelerate Apple's growth and expand its reach. A pivotal moment came when Jobs negotiated a deal with music industry executives to bring their content to the iTunes Store. By forging these partnerships, Apple was able to provide a seamless user experience and establish the iPod as the go-to music player, paving the way for the digital music revolution.

The story of Steve Jobs and Apple serves as a powerful point on the significance of partnerships in entrepreneurial success. From his early collaboration with Steve Wozniak to the creative alliances with Jonathan Ive and strategic partnerships with industry giants, Jobs understood that the collective genius of a team could achieve what an individual alone could not.

I say this with great conviction, the value of synergy cannot be underestimated in partnerships. It brings together diverse talents, fuels growth, sparks innovation, enhances efficiency, and propels success. When partners harness the power of synergy, they unlock the potential for extraordinary achievements and create a solid foundation for long-term collaboration and mutual benefit just like the success story of Apple Inc.

Nurturing Trust and Collaboration is essential for building strong and successful partnerships. When trust is present, partners can operate with confidence, transparency, and mutual respect, creating an environment that fosters collaboration and drives collective success.

Trust in a partnership begins with open communication and honesty. Each partner should feel comfortable expressing their thoughts, concerns, and ideas without fear of judgment or negative repercussions. By fostering a culture of open dialogue, partners can address challenges, share feedback, and work towards common solutions.

Collaboration, on the other hand, is all about working together towards shared objectives. It requires a mindset of shared responsibility and a willingness to listen, understand, and value the input of others. Effective collaboration involves leveraging each partner's strengths, expertise, and perspectives to achieve greater outcomes. By embracing a collaborative approach, you and your partners can tap into collective knowledge, experience synergistic benefits, and most importantly drive innovation.

Additionally, it is important to celebrate achievements and milestones together. Recognizing and appreciating the contributions of each partner strengthens the sense of collaboration and reinforces a positive working environment. By acknowledging successes, partners feel valued and motivated to continue working together towards shared goals.

Creating Mutually Beneficial Relationships

A strong partnership is a win-win situation for both parties involved. We will delve into the art of creating mutually beneficial relationships, where each partner contributes and receives value in equal measure. By understanding the needs, strengths, and aspirations of your partners, you can find ways to support and uplift each other, driving collective growth and success.

Creating mutually beneficial partnerships can serve as a pillar to fostering your relationship. When both parties derive value and advantages from the partnership, it fosters a sustainable and long-lasting collaboration. Such relationships are built on the principles of mutual respect, shared goals, and a commitment to supporting each other's growth and success.

To create a mutually beneficial relationship, it is crucial to establish a clear understanding of each partner's needs, objectives, and expectations. Open and honest communication is key in identifying areas of common interest and exploring how the partnership can address those needs. By aligning goals and expectations, partners can ensure that their collaboration is built on a solid foundation.

Lesson Learned

I absolutely love partnerships. Growing up in the Silicon Valley you're naturally around a lot of startups, as a young entrepreneur I recall many prelim conversations about ideas for a product or a service and who would be the best fit for a partner on this venture. Looking back every startup went into motion with their goal to be bigger than a mom-and-pop operation. And because of that, no one tried to go at their business plan alone.

Some years back, I landed a great opportunity with a company wanting to pay premium pricing for my collaboration for three months that could lead to a much longer duration if I wanted. I immediately thought of my long-time friend who had done business ventures in the past with me. I couldn't wait to bring her in as a partner with me. When word got out that I was bringing her on as a partner the raindrops of opinionated advice began to pour in. I had the:

1. *Sideways rain* that hits you no matter where you place your umbrella. These were the people that were personal friends of mine that were in my ear, telling me that the partnership was a bad idea, they felt that I had worked hard for my reputation that brought me these types of high paying contracts.

2. *Stop and go rain* that comes down then vanishes, then comes right back again. This represented the

colleagues that were already in a partnership and absolutely hated it. They would say things like, "Yeah, there are perks to having a partner, but think of all the money that you'll be making and then having to split it two ways." Or "what if you put in more work than the other partner and they're still getting the benefits."

3. Steady drizzle rain that keeps you indoors. This is your close circle that "is only looking out for your best interest", they are the ones that know best. They keep you reminded of what everyone else is saying and any doubts that you may expressed about the partnership. They pump you up like your internal cheer team, highlighting all your accomplishments and how you have these magical superpowers that have no room for a partner. They give you the confidence that you can actually tackle this big goal all by yourself.

4. *Foggy rain*, the rain is obstructing the view ahead. This is your own internal battle, where you're trying hard to have your own opinion about the idea you came up with to partner in the first place. You weigh in all the data of opinions and put it up against how you're feeling about the situation now. At this point your excitement about partnering has diminished and doesn't stand a chance.

This is what happened to me.

I allowed everyone else's facts, traumas, failures, and jealousy of my potential partner to derail me from my own facts. The whole reason why I wanted to have a partner in the first place.

- She had a skillset that wasn't natural for me.

- She knew how I operated, and we worked as one.

- I loved being around her and never got tired or annoyed.
- I was a single mom of five kids, challenged with time capacity.
- She was brilliant when it came to her area of expertise.
- Together we created synergy.

This was a big lesson learned, so I decided to stay solo. Sure, it felt great at first, especially because everyone believed in me so much, but it was exhausting, and I ran myself ragged doing it. By the time the three months were up, I wanted to be done with it and close that chapter. I look back and know without a shadow of a doubt that deal would have turned into something so great had I just listened to my internal voice. Not only did I lose out on the true potential of the project at hand, but I put a strain on my relationship with my friend by not putting my faith and trust in what we were committed to doing together.

I have had many partnerships since then, and nobody's opinion penetrates over my own facts and logic. Trusting in myself and who I have selected to partner with has served me well from that point on.

Ask Yourself This

If others are telling me it's a bad idea, unpack their feelings about it and decide if they have valid points.

What plan does the opinionated party have in place to support my business moving forward in place of the partner you originally selected?

What experience does the opinionated party have to support their opinion against the proposed partnership? Do they run their own business?

These questions, when not explored, are typically what hold people back from joining forces with partners that could lead to greater success collectively than independently. No matter what I do, whether it be business or personal I thrive as a partner and collaborator. I never want to be a solopreneur, EVER. United, we can do anything. As a singular entity we are limited and isolated.

A crucial aspect of creating a mutually beneficial relationship is to seek out a win-win outcome. This means striving for solutions and agreements that provide advantages and benefits to all parties involved. Think of your partnership as a marriage, focusing on creating value for both sides, the partnership becomes more sustainable, resilient and can overcome any obstacle together.

Flexibility and adaptability are also essential in maintaining a mutually beneficial relationship. Business landscapes and circumstances can change over time, and it is important to be open to adjusting the terms of the partnership to accommodate these changes. Regular communication and periodic reviews of the partnership's effectiveness can help identify areas for improvement and ensure that both parties continue to derive value from the collaboration.

Trust and transparency are vital elements in building and nurturing mutually beneficial relationships. Each partner should feel confident in sharing information, insights, and resources with the understanding that they will be used for the collective benefit of the partnership. Trust fosters collaboration and encourages the exchange of these ideas and knowledge, leading to innovative solutions and mutual growth.

Managing and Resolving Conflicts

Conflict is inevitable in any partnership, but how you navigate and resolve conflicts can make or break the relationship. We will explore effective conflict management strategies, emphasizing the importance of open dialogue, empathy, and compromise. By proactively addressing conflicts and finding mutually agreeable solutions, you can strengthen your partnerships and build resilience for the long haul.

Managing and resolving conflicts is an essential skill in any partnership, as disagreements and differences of opinion are inevitable. Effectively addressing conflicts can strengthen the relationship and lead to better outcomes. Here are some key considerations for managing and resolving conflicts in partnerships:

Open Communication

Encourage open and honest communication between partners. Create a safe space where each party feels comfortable expressing their concerns, sharing their perspectives, and actively listening to one another. Clear and respectful communication is crucial in understanding the root causes of conflicts and finding mutually agreeable solutions.

Active Listening

Practice active listening by giving full attention to the other party's viewpoints and concerns. Seek to understand their perspective without judgment or interruption. By demonstrating empathy and showing that you value their input, you can foster an environment of mutual respect and collaboration.

Focus on Interests

Instead of getting caught up in positions or specific demands, focus on identifying the underlying interests of each party. By understanding the motivations and needs behind their positions, you can explore alternative solutions that address those interests and find common ground.

Collaborative Problem-Solving

Encourage a problem-solving mindset where both parties work together to find mutually beneficial solutions. Brainstorm ideas, explore different options, and consider the potential impact of each solution on both sides. By involving all stakeholders in the process, you increase the likelihood of finding resolutions that satisfy everyone involved.

Mediation and Facilitation

In more complex or intense conflicts, consider involving a neutral third party to facilitate the resolution process. A mediator can help guide the discussion, encourage constructive communication, and offer unbiased perspectives. Their objective is to help both parties reach a mutually agreeable resolution that aligns with their interests.

Constructive Conflict Resolution

Encourage a focus on resolving conflicts rather than winning arguments. Emphasize the importance of finding common ground and maintaining a long-term relationship. Encourage compromise, flexibility, and creative problem-solving to find solutions that address the core issues and maintain the overall health of the partnership.

Remember, conflicts are natural in any collaborative endeavor. How they are managed and resolved can make a significant difference in the success and sustainability of a partnership. By promoting open communication, active listening, collaborative problem-solving, and a focus on mutual interests, conflicts can be transformed into opportunities for greater understanding, collaboration, and growth.

Now that we have explored the transformative potential of partnerships and their role in building a sustainable and thriving business. By embracing the principles of synergy, trust, mutual benefit, conflict management, and long-term cultivation, you can forge partnerships that endure and contribute to the long-term success of your entrepreneurial journey. Remember, strong alliances are not just about short-term gains but about building a network of support, collaboration, and shared growth. As you embark on your partnership-building journey, may you find the right allies to join you in creating a legacy that extends far beyond your individual efforts.

Case Study Analysis

Read the case study about Steve Jobs and Apple Inc. and answer the following questions:

a. How did Steve Jobs utilize partnerships to drive the success of Apple?

b. What were some of the key partnerships that contributed to Apple's growth and innovation?

c. What lessons can be learned from Steve Jobs' approach to partnerships?

Partnership Evaluation

Imagine you are considering forming a partnership for your business. Identify five potential partners who align with your vision and mission. For each potential partner, evaluate and analyze their strengths, complementary skills, and how they align with your goals. Consider the potential synergy and benefits that can be achieved through the partnership.

Conflict Resolution Plan

Develop a conflict resolution plan for managing conflicts that may arise in a partnership. Outline strategies for open communication, active listening, focusing on interests, collaborative problem-solving, and, if needed, the involvement of a neutral third party.

Partnership Decision

Make a list of five reasons why you would hesitate to partner with someone and five reasons why you would consider partnering with them. Reflect on your own business situation and determine if it would be beneficial to bring on a partner based on the criteria you have outlined.

Remember to provide thoughtful and detailed responses for each task, be obsessed about the design and intricate detail of your business.

Take Action

Reflection Questions:

a. Am I doing this business to create a well-off lifestyle or because I am solving a need in the market?

b. How big do I want to scale my business?

c. What skill set should I look for in a potential partner?

d. Am I afraid to share prosperity?

e. Do I like the spotlight of the business's innovative ideas?

f. If others are telling me it's a bad idea, unpack their feelings about it and decide if they have valid points.

Notes

Notes

[CH 10] Igniting Your Entrepreneurial Journey

Congratulations, you've embarked on an incredible journey through the pages of this book, uncovering the secrets to crafting your very own Entrepreneurial Empire. As you stand at the precipice of this final chapter, I want you to know that your dreams are valid, your aspirations are within reach, and your potential is limitless. You've absorbed insights, strategies, and wisdom, and now it's time to channel all that energy into creating your own path of impact.

Your experience in entrepreneurship is not just a collection of successes and failures; it's a reservoir of power waiting to be harnessed. Every trial, every victory, every moment of doubt and determination has shaped you into the resilient individual you are today. And now, armed with the knowledge you've gained, you have the capacity to transform challenges into opportunities, to turn setbacks into stepping stones towards your empire.

Remember, entrepreneurship isn't about following a predetermined formula; it's about embracing your authenticity. Your unique journey, your voice, your vision – they're your most potent assets. In a world of noise, be the voice that resonates with authenticity, because people are drawn to those who bring genuine value.

As you set out to solve problems in your chosen market space, keep in mind that your experiences, your passions, and your quirks are the very essence that sets you apart. Your customers don't just want another product or service; they want your perspective, your insight, and your unwavering commitment and conviction, delivering something that resonates with them deeply. It's perfectly okay to infuse your business with your true self. Authenticity breeds connection, and connection is the foundation of loyalty. The value you bring isn't just about transactions; it's about the transformation you create in the lives of your customers. They're not just buying your product; they're investing in your journey, your story, and the promise of something better. Your story is your superpower!

So, here's my heartfelt message to you: go out and be the FORCE of innovation you've discovered within yourself. Embrace the uncertainty, the late nights, and the challenges as part of your growth story. Turn every experience – good or bad – into fuel that propels you forward, blazing your path so bright that people near and far will gather around you. Your path will have moments of doubt and difficulty, trust me I know them well, but let those moments be reminders that growth will always sprout up beyond our comfort zones. Trust the process, and most importantly trust in yourself. You have the tools, the knowledge, and the resilience to tackle anything that comes your way. We got this!

Let us not forget that our entrepreneurial journey is both a personal and collective adventure. Reach out to mentors, partners, and fellow entrepreneurs. Collaborate, share, and lift each other up. The Empirical Empire you're building isn't just for you; it's part of the vibrant tapestry of innovation that fuels progress and change, builds community, and lifts those around us. As you step into this new chapter of your life, embrace the challenges, uncertainties, and opportunities with an open heart and fierce determination. Your story, your business, and your impact are already unfolding in ways you might not yet fathom. Your journey is uniquely yours, and it's time to let your brilliance shine, to create, to innovate, and to make a mark that resonates through time, and beyond you.

Remember, you're not alone on this path. You've joined a community of doers, shakers and visionaries who are transforming the world one idea at a time. Embrace your power, your authenticity, and your purpose. You have the potential to ignite change, to build empires, and to leave a legacy that inspires generations to come. Now go out there and let your Entrepreneurial Empire rise. The world is ready for the magic that only you can create. Your journey has just begun, and with every step forward, you're shaping a future that's not just successful but impactful, not just meaningful but extraordinary.

Let's Stay Connected

This is where our new relationship begins to blossom. Where the power of collective ambition converges to illuminate your path to triumph. This is not just a chapter's end; it's the prologue to your most exhilarating ventures that are waiting to be experienced.

Join the community of the Entrepreneurial Empire where you are not a solitary warrior; you're a cherished member of our community that champions your ascent. Entrepreneurial Empire isn't just an entity; it's a resounding champion for your conquests, a guiding light in moments of uncertainty, and a steadfast hand that launches you forward.

As you stand on the cusp of transformation, remember that your challenges don't define you; they refine you. This journey isn't about mere techniques; it's about crafting a resilient mindset that blazes through adversity, both in your personal life and professional endeavors.

Let's Take Action.

Join the Entrepreneurial Empire Community and Fuel Your Success Journey!

Are you ready to transform your journey into an empire? Join our vibrant community on social media and unlock a world of techniques, insights, and resources that will rocket your business forward.

Here's your invitation to connect with a tribe of like-minded trailblazers, passionate about turning their creativity into reality.

Why Join Our Community?

 Stay Informed

Gain access to the latest industry trends, strategies, and best practices that will keep you ahead of the curve. Our community is a hub of knowledge that empowers you to make informed decisions for your business.

 Network and Collaborate

Connect with fellow entrepreneurs, business leaders, and experts who share your passion and drive. Collaborate, share experiences, and create meaningful partnerships that could be the catalyst for your next big success.

💥 Resource Hub

Our community is a treasure trove of resources – from expert conversations and guides to webinars and exclusive content, along with engaging events that bring the community together. You'll find everything you need to navigate the challenges and seize the opportunities that come your way.

📣 Engage and Interact

Participate in engaging discussions, ask questions, and receive valuable insights from seasoned professionals and fellow entrepreneurs. This is your platform to voice your thoughts and learn from others.

How to Join

1. **Follow Us:** Instagram @Entrepreneurial_Empire_

2. **Stay updated** with our posts, updates, and announcements.

3. **Engage:** Like, share, and comment on our posts to engage with the community and contribute to meaningful conversations.

4. **Connect:** Connect with fellow members, start conversations, and make lasting connections that will enrich your entrepreneurial journey.

5. **Stay Curious:** Keep an eye out for our regular updates, events, and resources that will provide you with actionable insights to drive your business forward.

Are you ready to be part of a community that shares your passion for entrepreneurship and growth? Join the Entrepreneurial Empire community today and start your journey towards building your empire of success. Together, we'll conquer new heights and turn our dreams into realities. I can't wait to hear all about what you're doing and would love to cheer you on.

See you there!

Notes

Notes

About the Author

Your Entrepreneurial Empire journey starts now! Embrace your potential, command your growth, and seize the reins of industry dominance. Your success story is being cultivated on every page of this book.

Prepare to be inspired and empowered by the dynamic force that is Jacqueline N. Hernandez. As CEO and Founder of Entrepreneurial Empire LLC Coaching and Consulting firm, host of Entrepreneurial Empire podcast, she is a seasoned entrepreneur, organizational development expert, visionary and mom of five. Jacqueline is living proof that dreams can be turned into reality with unwavering determination.

With over 17 years of experience in the Learning and Development space and organizational growth, Jacqueline's journey is a testament to the power of ambition and resilience. Hailing from the heart of Silicon Valley, she's not just a witness to innovation; she's a driving force behind it.

Her accolades aren't just accolades – they're milestones marking her incredible journey. From gracing the "Celebrity Apprentice" show season 8 episode 4, as a guest judge to captivating audiences as a guest interviewee on The American Dreams Radio Show hosted by Alan Olsen (the managing partner at GROCO Advisors to the Ultra Affluent, or leading Silicon Valley Business Summits and conference, along with many keynote opportunities, where her insights and expertise have caught the attention of industry giants. She has worked with start-ups, network marketing companies, government agencies, non-profits, ultra-affluent families and fortune 100 companies all to become the authority in an authentic arena.

But it's not just about recognition; it's about her relentless pursuit of excellence. Jacqueline's innate ability to tackle challenges head-on, from strategic planning to project management, has propelled her to a league of her own. She's a change-maker, a motivator, and a trailblazer of innovation.

Her unique ability to harmonize her role as a mother and an entrepreneur is the cohesion for her mantra "no excuses". She embodies the spirit of a mompreneur who's not only shaping her business but also nurturing a thriving family. Her journey serves as a shining example of how work-life balance isn't just a concept

With her experience she is here to guide you to the top of the mountain that stands before you. Her journey is a beacon of hope, a blueprint for success, and a call to action for those who refuse to settle for mediocrity. Whether you're a budding entrepreneur or a parent seeking to strike that elusive balance, Jacqueline's story will ignite your passion and push you to take the leap.

Join her on this exhilarating journey of entrepreneurship, family, and growth. Embrace the energy, seize the opportunities, and become a part of Jacqueline's legacy as she continues to create empires through vision, action, and an unshakeable belief. The time to unleash your potential is in the pages of this book.

https://bit.ly/-focused-action